Praise for John Schlimm:

FOR *GRILLING VEGAN STYLE:*

"Grilling Vegan Style cracks the code to making summer last all year round by combining equal parts compassion, fire, and nature's freshest ingredients. This is a feast the whole family can enjoy, and feel good about!"

—GENE BAUR, PRESIDENT AND CO-FOUNDER OF FARM SANCTUARY

"We often cite several inspirations for what we do at MATT & NAT, however few of them get us salivating as does great vegan food! John's pioneering take on the traditional BBQ in Grilling Vegan Style *(including desserts!) has gotten us VERY excited. Another cultural phenomenon has been brought into the twenty-first century, thank you John for providing vegans a path to partake in a favorite summertime tradition!"*

—INDER BEDI, FOUNDER AND CREATIVE DIRECTOR OF MATT & NAT

"I have to admit that I was a little skeptical about a Vegan Grilling book. After all in my world it's all about the meat. I might even be considered a Non-Vegan! But John's book has opened my eyes to the concept and his recipes are outstanding. The Slip-N-Sliders is a great recipe for everyone and I guarantee I'm going to try the Strawberry Skewers with Vanilla, I Scream! real soon!"

—RAY LAMPE AKA DR. BBQ, AUTHOR OF *RIBS, CHOPS, STEAKS, AND WINGS*
AND *DR. BBQ's BIG-TIME BARBECUE COOKBOOK*

"I dare you to flip through this book and not already start to daydream about which mouth-watering recipe you'd use to wow your friends at the next backyard BBQ. I can't decide who would be more fun to grill for: hipster gourmands on a rooftop in Brooklyn or my veganophobic friends in my dad's backyard in Indiana. The recipes in this book are equal opportunity wowers!"

—MARISA MILLER WOLFSON, WRITER AND DIRECTOR OF *VEGUCATED*

"Grilling Vegan Style brings you the best of all possible worlds—delicious, fun foods prepared in the most healthful way. For everyone who loves grilling, this is the way to do it right."

—BARNARD, MD, PRESIDENT OF THE PHYSICIANS
COMMITTEE FOR RESPONSIBLE MEDICINE

"When I was a kid, the best thing in the world was grilling time. Grilling Vegan Style brings the nostalgia back and highlights that for me as a new dad, there is a way to share the ritual of 'food and fire' with my son."

—BIZ STONE, CO-FOUNDER OF TWITTER AND OBVIOUS

FOR *THE TIPSY VEGAN:*

"Thanks to The Tipsy Vegan, I now have a lot more fun eating my vegetables! John's recipes are incredibly delicious, inspired, fun to make and eat. It's truly good mood food!"

—ERIN MCKENNA, CHEF AND FOUNDER OF BABYCAKES NYC,
AUTHOR OF *BABYCAKES* AND *BABYCAKES COVERS THE CLASSICS*

"In this fun book, John Schlimm makes vegan cuisine the life of the party. Easy to make, the recipes are healthy—with a kick!"

—ELIZABETH FALKNER, CHEF, ORSON AND CITIZEN CAKE,
AUTHOR OF *DEMOLITION DESSERTS*

"Exploding conventional stereotypes of vegan cooking, The Tipsy Vegan *takes the compassionate lifestyle to the next level. The menus in this uproariously fun cookbook exude the flair of a true 'bon viveur.'"*

—Colleen Patrick-Goudreau, best-selling author of *Color Me Vegan*, *Vegan's Daily Companion*, and *The 30-Day Vegan Challenge*

"The Tipsy Vegan *is the ideal way to eat your way to inebriation of the most delicious kind. And to think I can tell everyone that you named this tasty collection after me—the 'Tip'sy vegan. This book is a tempting tribute to the animals—and they thank you for it—So do I."*

—Tippi Hedren, president of the Roar Foundation, shambala.org

"*John Schlimm's clever and kind cookbook* The Tipsy Vegan *is a boozy and compassionate good time just waiting to happen. Cheers!"*

—Todd Oldham, designer and author

"*Whether you fancy yourself an average chug-a-lug beer drinker, an occasional cocktail drinker, or a fine wine connoisseur, without a doubt you'll find several recipes in this book to tantalize your taste buds."*

—Beverly Lynn Bennett, www.veganchef.com

"The Tipsy Vegan *smashes to smithereens the morbid myth that vegans are dour and joyless. It gives us recipes to gratify any lover of good food; that they carry a little kick is simply a delightful bonus."*

—Victoria Moran, author of *Main Street Vegan* and *Creating a Charmed Life*

"*I didn't realize veganism can be so fun. A delightful, smart, and elegant read,* The Tipsy Vegan *offers a cornucopia of culinary adventures, hiccups included."*

—Farmer John Peterson, founder of Angelic Organics and star of *The Real Dirt on Farmer John*

FOR *THE SEVEN STARS COOKBOOK*:

"*Gambling, sex, and rock 'n' roll. What do these have to do with food? Everything! And* The Seven Stars Cookbook *nails all of the above."*

—Jackie Collins

"*Caesars Entertainment has it all—amazing casinos, good food, fabulous people, and now a really great cookbook!"*

—Rocco Dispirito

"*There is something for everyone with these great recipe selections from the fabulous lineup of the world's finest chefs. Make yourself a winner in the kitchen and certainly in the dining room as you work your way through each and every delectable recipe."*

—Paul Prudhomme

"*Full of down-home—and delicious recipes—that we'd all love to have!"*

—John Besh

Other books by John Schlimm:

The Tipsy Vegan

Twang: a novel

The Seven Stars Cookbook

The Ultimate Beer Lover's Cookbook

The Beer Lover's Cookbook

The Pennsylvania Celebrities Cookbook

Straub Brewery

The Straub Beer Party Drinks Handbook

The Straub Beer Cookbook

Corresponding with History

GRILLING Vegan STYLE

125 FIRED-UP RECIPES TO TURN EVERY BITE INTO A BACKYARD BBQ

JOHN SCHLIMM

PHOTOGRAPHS BY AMY BEADLE ROTH

Da Capo
LIFE LONG
A Member of the Perseus Books Group

Library of Congress Cataloging-in-Publication Data

Schlimm, John E., 1971–
  Grilling vegan style!: 125 fired-up recipes to turn every bite into a backyard BBQ / John Schlimm ; photographs by Amy Beadle Roth.
     p. cm.
  Includes bibliographical references and index.
  ISBN 978-0-7382-1572-3 (pbk. : alk. paper) – ISBN 978-0-7382-1583-9 (e-book) 1. Vegan cooking. 2. Barbecuing. 3. Vegetarian cooking. 4. Cookbooks. I. Title.
  TX837.S313 2012
  641.7'6--dc23

                          2011040309

First Da Capo Press edition 2012

Published by Da Capo Press
A Member of the Perseus Books Group
www.dacapopress.com

Design and production by Megan Jones Design (www.meganjonesdesign.com)

Note: The information in this book is true and complete to the best of our knowledge. This book is intended only as an informative guide for those wishing to know more about health issues. In no way is this book intended to replace, countermand, or conflict with the advice given to you by your own physician. The ultimate decision concerning care should be made between you and your doctor. We strongly recommend you follow his or her advice. Information in this book is general and is offered with no guarantees on the part of the authors or Da Capo Press. The authors and publisher disclaim all liability in connection with the use of this book.

Da Capo Press books are available at special discounts for bulk purchases in the U.S. by corporations, institutions, and other organizations. For more information, please contact the Special Markets Department at the Perseus Books Group, 2300 Chestnut Street, Suite 200, Philadelphia, PA, 19103, or call (800) 810-4145, ext. 5000, or e-mail special.markets@perseusbooks.com.

10 9 8 7 6 5 4 3 2 1

To All the Animals—
So you know that you have not passed
this way unloved.

"I have only one burning desire
Let me stand next to your fire"

—Jimi Hendrix

Contents

Chapter 6

TAPAS ON THE DECK 87

Chapter 7

COUNTRY MARINADES FOR
TOFU, TEMPEH & SEITAN 103

Chapter 8

THE BURGERS ARE READY! 121

Chapter 9

THE NEW TAILGATING CLASSICS 143

Chapter 10

SUPPER UNDER THE STARS

Chapter 11

PICNIC DESSERTS

Chapter 12

GRILLSIDE HAPPY HOUR

Introduction

WE HAVE BEEN playing with fire and food since the dawn of civilization, when the earliest form of grilling was born of necessity and survival over the very first roaring flames just outside the cave. Thousands of years later, this outdoor ritual has become a bona fide art form, and the domain of backyard hosts and hostesses who revel in turning up the heat to roll out an unforgettable feast the old-fashioned way while dazzling wide-eyed guests.

Grilling Vegan Style now moves the grill another step forward into a new era of revelry and entertaining, while still embracing the nostalgia of what it has always really been about.

The grill is more than just a big metal box that springs to life with the strike of a match or push of a button. It's as much a state of mind as it is a place where we escape to, where we share our lives over rounds of ice-cold beer and cocktails. The grill is where time is counted not in minutes or years, but rather, in burgers and corncobs and laughter. What follows is a lively garden of many flavors, which are marked just as much by an adventurous spirit as they are infused with compassion and awareness.

For many people, *grill* is synonymous with *meat*. But not anymore. Grilling just got a whole lot tastier and friendlier. Did you know you can grill salads and sandwiches? And even desserts? Whether in the backyard, at the beach, or hanging out in the middle of nowhere, consider this your official handbook for eating your way to the grilled life with family and friends. Throughout this book, in addition to giving you more than 125 recipes,

I lay out the tools and basics of firing up as well as explain the various grilling techniques for everything from tofu, tempeh, and seitan to a wide array of vegetables and fruits that I bet you never thought of tossing on the barbie before, but now you will again and again. This is information you can also use to make your own original creations hot off the grill anytime you want.

You're about to experience some of your favorite ingredients and a bunch of new ones as you've never seen them before: flame-kissed and raring to party. And the only thing cruel about getting fired up at this bash is running out of charcoal or gas before you finish making Cedar-Smoked Mushrooms, Slip-N-Sliders, or Spicy Corn with Black Beans & Zucchini.

These pages are where grill meets vegan—and falls madly in love. We are blazing new trails in this celebration where all are welcome grillside, whether you're a lifelong vegan, a newbie, an occasional visitor, or simply hungry. In fact, veterans of the grill circuit as well as those lighting up here for the very first time will both find recipes to pique your interest, tempt your palate, and inspire you to new levels of fiery "grate"-ness. Tattooed Watermelon Salad, anyone?

The dishes you're about to enjoy are more about great-tasting food than what is or is not on the ingredient list. If you dig *caliente*, then head for the Shiny Happy Poppers or Drop It like It's Hot Sauce. If you're looking for traditional with a twist, hit up the burger chapter and take a bite of the Mexican Tortilla Burger or Italian Herb Burger with a side of Flame Day Fries. During tailgating season, cheer on the home team with Halftime Pizza, Seventh Inning Stretch Tacos, and a Blooming Onion with Sauce on the Sidelines.

For light bites, salads, and tapas, impress your guests with the likes of Shishito Heat Wave, Party on South Peach Salsa, Sweet Potato & Green Onion Country Salad, and Artichokes with Cumin Dipping Sauce. Then sit down to supper under the stars with Zucchinicotti, Veggie Quesadillas with Sparky Corn Relish, Starry Night Tart, or a DIY kebab bar with an entire chapter's worth of marinades. And for dessert—*oh, the desserts!* Grilled Peaches with Raspberry Sauce, Vanilla Pound Cake, and Strawberry Skewers all scream "summer" by the mouthful.

Of course, it wouldn't be much of a party without thirst quenchers for all your guests: perhaps the Six-Pack Punch or A Pitcher of Margaritas for the adults, and Watermelon Giggles or a Frozen Tootie Fruity Good Moody Cutie for the youngsters.

Rain, shine, or blizzard, the grill knows no boundaries. Now you, too, are ready to entertain year-round with dishes that are easy to prepare and what I like to call small-town friendly, meaning anyone, anywhere can grill up a storm (even inside, thanks to the invention of the grill pan!). My buddies at home and my big-city pals alike can all head out to their local grocery stores and farmers' markets, and find just what they need for these recipes.

When I do introduce special ingredients, such as vegan chocolate (to once and for all prove S'More Is Always Better!) or vegan versions of cheese, sour cream, mayonnaise, and Worcestershire sauce, I also provide either door-to-door online sources or homemade versions you can quickly whip up. After all, *ease* has always been grilling's middle name.

My favorite part about a barbecue is that everyone gets involved. A few people rinse, peel, and chop while someone else readies the grill. Another sets the table as various ones bustle back and forth with armfuls of bowls, platters, and condiments. And still another has the all-important task of mixing the cocktails. Then the grill master assumes his or her position amid this happy orbit of family and friends, and performs what can only be described as pure magic. This is how a meal is meant to be savored—slowly and together.

My friends, I now invite you to join me for a feast thousands of years in the making. Together around this grill, we paramours of life lived to the absolute fullest will kick back, laugh, raise our glasses, and eat to our hearts' content!

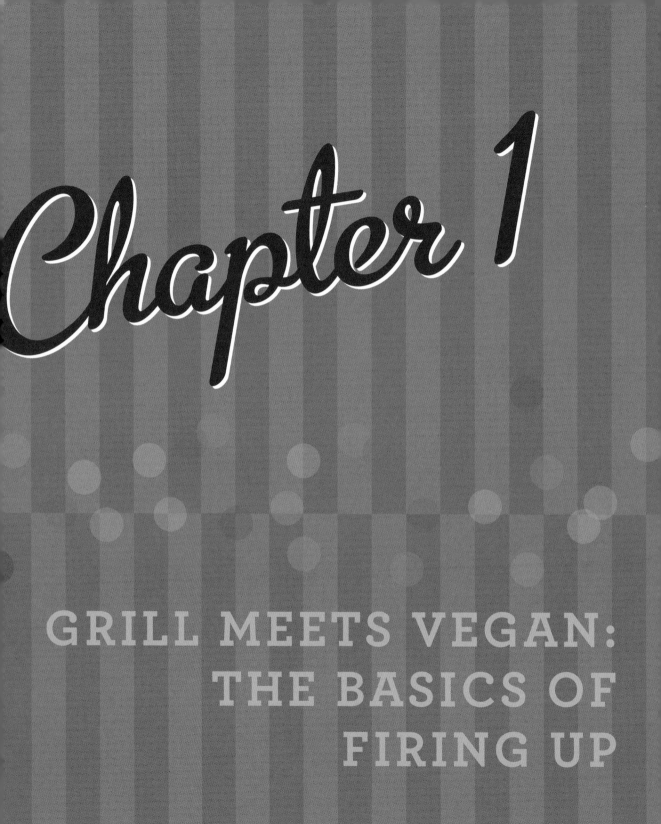

Chapter 1

GRILL MEETS VEGAN: THE BASICS OF FIRING UP

You may already know your way around the grill, or perhaps you are unwrapping your grill pan for the first time or wondering what the best way to light charcoal is. Maybe you've never heard of a chimney starter or grill basket before, or you're curious about what the best type of skewer is for kebabs. And how does a mountain pie maker fit into all of this?

Regardless of where you're at in your grilling adventures, this chapter offers practical tips for grilling and maintaining heat levels, discussion of the different types of grills available, descriptions of popular and necessary grilling tools, and an overall introduction to the basics that will ease you into the exciting world of grilling and the recipes that follow, ensuring you always have a great time when firing up.

GETTING STARTED

Let's begin with the grill itself. When it comes to finding the best one for you, do your research. Don't settle for the first model you see. Comparison shop, check out different brands and models in stores and online (see the list on page 221), and ask fellow grillers for their input and recommendations. After all, buying a grill is an investment for which you'll want an abundant return of good memories, laughter, and unforgettable meals for many years to come.

When searching for your dream grill, make sure the construction is solid with no wiggle room (literally). Stainless-steel grills are a good choice for the long haul.

Look for a grill with a cast-iron or stainless-steel grate, or other type that is strong and will not rust.

Regarding what size grill to buy, decide where the grill will be used and if it will be used for small family dinners only or also larger parties. A deluxe grill with all the bells and whistles in the store looks great until you get it home and it overtakes your porch or patio. Likewise, will the grill be used in one location, or moved around the yard per your entertaining needs? If you plan on having a mobile grill, then a manageable size and wheels are recommended, as opposed to a large, bulky grill or built-in version. Or maybe you simply want a small hibachi that you can take with you on the road. Something else to consider when thinking about size and location is that you will need to place your grill on level ground, whether it's on a deck or patio, or on grass or sand. This will ensure the grill works properly and evenly heats your food.

If you plan on grilling when the sun goes down, make sure to place your grill in a well-lit area. There are such things as grill lights, and they come in a variety of shapes and sizes, all meant to light up your world.

When it comes to grills, size does matter (a little anyway). The larger the grilling area, the more room you'll have to move food around from direct to indirect heat (see page 10), as well as more room to play and experiment with these recipes. Likewise, be careful not to overcrowd your grill surface. Even a small amount of space between items on the grill will further ensure even cooking. Also, it's always a good idea to leave a fire-free area on the grate surface, perhaps to one side, should any food need a quick cooldown.

A grill with additional counter space attached is recommended, allowing for last-minute prep outside, and extra space also provides easy access to food, seasonings, marinades, utensils, and other items while grilling. Or have a nearby table designated for this purpose. You can never have too much space when grilling.

Keep the grate well oiled with canola oil, vegetable oil, or another neutral-flavored oil. Use a basting brush, which is solely dedicated to this one task, to apply the oil to the grate after cleaning it and/or right before using it. Be sure to do this when the grate is cool to the touch. The oil will help prevent food from sticking to the grate and it will make for an easier cleanup. Even if not specifically mentioned in the following recipes, this is a good habit to get into. Furthermore, after careful cleaning, a grill pan also benefits from a light brushing with oil before being put away.

Master the *mise en place*! Or what we might call for our purposes, *mise en grill*. This is the professional chef's lingo for having everything from your grilling gear to the ingredients ready to go well before you get fired up. An organized griller is a happy one, and so are the hungry guests.

Fired-up grills *love* attention (some more than others). While grilling, stick close to the grill so you can monitor heat levels, cooking times, potential flare-ups, and any other issues that arise. Grilling is no time to run inside to answer the phone or head to the fridge for something you forgot.

Contrary to what some will say, frequently flipping your food on the grill is not a bad thing. After all, you're going for an even sizzle factor on all sides. Best rule of thumb: Follow the recipe, but follow your instincts, too. Different grills may have different effects on food, regardless of what the recipe says. Yet one more reason you and your grill should be connected at the hip during cooking time.

When it comes to cleaning, think of your grill as you would your stovetop and clean it after every use. This way, it will be ready the next time you want to grill and the food will taste better. For easy cleanup, shine up your grill with baking soda and water, to avoid using chemical-heavy cleaning products. Sprinkle baking soda on the grill, including the grate, and scrub with a damp sponge. Or for an especially dirty grate, make a thick paste with near equal parts baking soda and water, and have at it with a wire scrub brush. In both cases, rinse all with fresh water when finished. The best time to clean a grill is right after you're done cooking, allowing any remaining food particles to easily fall or wipe away. You should then clean the grill again before cooking the next time.

After every use, protect your grill with a weatherproof cover (see page 9). But be absolutely, positively, beyond a shadow of a doubt sure that your grill is turned off and is completely cooled down before covering it for the night. (I have a few friends who learned this lesson the hard way. Cue the fire extinguishers!)

SAFETY FIRST

When it comes to grilling, safety always comes first! While all the information in this book is geared toward a safe, happy, and memorable grilling experience, here are a few extra safety tips to keep in mind:

- Position your grill several feet from the side of your house and away from any shrubbery or plants.

- Grills give off carbon monoxide. So place your grill where there's good ventilation; never use the grill inside the house or on a deck/patio/other area covered by a roof or tree limbs. Only grills that are specified for indoor use should ever find their way into your home sweet home.

- Place a fireproof grill pad or patio protector or heavy sheet of metal under the grill to protect your deck or patio (see page 9).

- Keep children and pets away from the grill.

- Wear closed-toe shoes when grilling, lest any hot coals or sparks hop overboard.

- Have a dry chemical fire extinguisher close by, charged and ready to go just in case you need it (see page 9). And make sure you know how to use it. It also doesn't hurt to have a nearby water source, such as a hose or outdoor sink.

- Prevent *all* burns: Don't forget to put on your sunblock, hat, and sunglasses while grilling outside.

TYPES OF GRILLS

Luckily for us grilling junkies, finding the perfect grill to fit our needs has become easier than ever. Whether we're a prince or pauper, daily grill master or weekend grill warrior, there's a grill waiting out there for each one of us.

For the recipes in this book, you don't need any particular type of grill. Therefore, you must first decide what type of grill best suits your lifestyle. From there you can then move on to the really fun choices, such as size, color, accessories, and most important, which of the following recipes to treat yourself and your guests to next.

Charcoal Grills

Nothing conjures images of summer and wows the taste buds like the smell of a charcoal grill doing its thing, especially in the middle of winter. Although for decades charcoal grills have reigned as the lords of Grill Town, they have long found themselves embroiled in the ongoing debate of Team Charcoal vs. Team Gas, and now we might add Team Electric and Team Grill Pan to that mix.

To their benefit, charcoal grills are often cheaper to buy than the competition, burn hotter, offer the griller the option of using charcoal and/or wood, the resulting masterpieces have that classic smoky flavor, and let's face it—they're old-school cool!

On the flip side, a truly dedicated relationship with a charcoal grill requires constant attention, can be messy, is more expensive in the end, and is unpredictable, with heat levels changing from one minute to the next. The overachievers and romantics among us will surely embrace these challenges in the name of tradition and authentic flavor. As for everyone else, you may want to skip ahead to gas or electric grills and get right to business.

When it comes time to go shopping, you'll quickly discover that charcoal grills come in many shapes and sizes, usually as round, square, or oblong containers topped with a metal grate. Three of the most popular types of charcoal grills include the following:

Weber Kettle Grill: Simplicity is this famous grill's word on the street. For more than sixty years, the kettle grill with its domed top has been a symbol of backyard Americana, and the benchmark for charcoal grilling. Its vintage 1950s bowl shape set atop a steely tripod has compelled millions to ignite the coals and transform their backyard, deck, patio, and sandy getaway into party central.

Hibachi: Small and portable, the Japanese-inspired hibachi is a metal firebox with a grate that allows for easy and intimate grilling anywhere, especially for small items such as kebabs. For the best durability, choose a cast-iron version, and also consider weight in conjunction with how you plan to use it, such as taking it on road trips and to picnics. The show-offs among us (you know who you are!) can even set a hibachi on the outdoor table to really entertain a circle of family and friends during prep time. Or, if you're super limited on space (and can only fire up, say, on a small porch or balcony), a hibachi may be the thing for you.

Likewise, a close relative to the hibachi is the Yakatori tabletop grill. Small and constructed from fired ceramic clay for a more constant grilling temperature, the Yakatori tabletop grill mimics the traditional Japanese street grill design and is perfect for grilling kebabs and other small items. One go-to source for Yakatori tabletop grills is Well Traveled Living (www.wtliving.com), which offers the HotSpot Yakatori Charcoal Grill in both rectangular and circular tabletop designs.

Tuscan Grill: This is not a stand-alone grill, but rather one that requires a flame source. Grilling pioneers dating back centuries have used the Tuscan grill, which is a metal grate with sturdy legs that fits over a fire, or some version of it. These grills can be used over campfires or in fireplaces, which their namesake Tuscans and fellow Italians are fond of doing to this day. Cooking with a Tuscan grill or other type of grate used for grilling over a fire works best once the fire burns down to small flames and glowing embers, which allow for a more even heat source. This is a great way to "rough it" in the wilds.

The biggest consideration when choosing a traditional charcoal grill is the fact that it is less eco-friendly than its gas or electric counterparts because, for starters, it burns "dirty," leaving tiny soot particles in the air. But fear not; you can easily lessen the burden charcoal grilling places on you and Mother Nature.

Using natural and additive-free charcoal in place of charcoal briquettes (which often contain coal dust, sodium nitrate, borax, and other nasty stuff) or lump charcoal/charred wood (which adds greenhouse gases to the atmosphere and contributes to deforestation) will reduce the potentially harmful effects of charcoal grilling to you and your guests, and the environment. One big benefit readers of this book will immediately get to enjoy from charcoal grilling with these recipes is avoiding the polycyclic aromatic hydrocarbons (PAHs) and heterocyclic amines (HCAs), which are two kinds of potentially carcinogenic compounds that can form when grilling meat.

If using wood, steer clear of lumber scraps, painted/stained wood, chemically treated wood, softwoods such as pine, and other wood that appears questionable for any reason. Instead, use such popular hardwoods as apple, oak, beech, mesquite, hickory, maple, and cherry, or store-bought grilling wood chips. Your local hardware or outdoor store should be able to help you find the appropriate wood for your specific grilling needs.

Also, to start the fire, forgo the chemical-rich (and dangerous) lighter fluid, which sends carbon monoxide billowing into the air, and ignite the charcoals by using alternatives such as Fatwood Firestarter (www.fatwood.com), sawdust starters, paraffin starters, a chimney starter (see page 8), or an electric charcoal starter (see page 8).

Gas Grills

For the everyday griller who's on the move or who likes simple, clean, and easy outdoor entertaining, the gas grill fits the bill. In fact, a majority of the grilling faithful opt to get their parties started with this fiery wonder, which first emerged in the 1960s. Fueled by propane or natural gas at the push of a button, this is a cleaner, more efficient method of grilling than using charcoal, which is a determining factor for many grillers.

Gas grills vary in size and boast multiple burners, allowing different items to be cooked effortlessly at the same time and on their own terms. And, as with the hibachi, if you're limited for space, you need not be limited for grilling. Portable gas grills are particularly convenient, *and* eye catching, especially those with designs that make them look like they just landed from another planet.

When purchasing a gas grill, choose one with enough burners to fit your entertaining needs. A model with three or four burners is recommended (most have two to six). And make sure each burner has a separate control for multiple uses at the same time. Warming racks and side burners are also nice extras, as is attached counter space.

And for the aquatic-inclined grillers among us, there are even gas grills specifically designed for boats. Check out www.grillsforboats.com, www.iboats.com, and other sites for more information about grilling on lakes, rivers, and the high seas.

Electric Grills

If you're the type who prefers not to play with fire and likes to be plugged in, even when grilling, electric grills offer the thrill of grill marks minus the flame. Of course, that then means no live-fire flavor and often the inability to use indirect heat (see page 10).

Whereas electric grills come in all sizes great and small, countertop electric grills offer the convenience of grilling food inside if there isn't room outside for a larger grill, or during winter months when firing up the barbie might not be feasible for you. Electric grills also come in handy on balconies and areas where open flame cooking is prohibited.

Naturally, one main consideration when deciding whether to go electric is to be sure you have the necessary electrical outlet wherever you plan to use the grill, especially if outside, unless you're fond of rolling out a long extension cord every time you want to fire up.

Stovetop Grill Pans and Griddle

Some have called this invention "miraculous"! Made of a heavy metal such as cast iron or steel, or enameled, the dual grill pan and griddle is an easy choice for urbanites and others who either have no outdoor space for grilling or who prefer the comfort and convenience of their indoor kitchens.

Ranging from small to large, grill pans often have ridges on one side for achieving grill marks and are flat on the other side to serve as a griddle for pancakes. Grill pans are heated over a traditional stovetop, and are ready to roll at a moment's notice, grill marks included. As with any grill, you must decide how you plan to use the grill pan and what space you have available in order to determine the size and type you need.

Hybrid Grills

If you want the best of both worlds when it comes to grilling, hybrid grills offer the unique ability to grill using charcoal or wood and propane or natural gas in a variety of combinations over the same grate. For example, the gas burners can be used to ignite the charcoal and then be turned off for a full charcoal grilling experience, or used alone for convenience and less mess. While pricey, a hybrid grill has a certain twenty-first-century ring to it.

Kalamazoo Outdoor Gourmet (www.kalamazoogourmet.com/hybrid), which invented hybrid grilling technology, offers a variety of options, including freestanding and built-in outdoor hybrid grills. For warmer climates, especially where outdoor kitchens are more practical for easy year-round use, the built-in hybrid grill could be a wise investment that will pay off many times over in the years ahead.

Also a hybrid of sorts and very popular for its versatility is the dual-zone grill. This style grill, which has a gas grill and a charcoal grill connected side by side, is more widely available and less expensive than the pure hybrid variety. These duo gas and charcoal grills offer the flexibility of ease and smoky, charred tradition to satisfy all your outdoor cooking preferences.

TOOLS OF THE TRADE

Once you have your grill, it's time to accessorize. The popularity of grilling has translated into thousands of related products, some practical and necessary, whereas others are whimsical and all about the bragging rights. Ultimately, most grilling gear is meant to help you perform your cooking duties with ease and style.

While having grill baskets in every shape and size or dozens of decorative kebab skewers isn't exactly a necessity, the following are items that every griller should have handy.

Grilling Gloves

Here's a newsflash: Grills get hot—*really* hot. Protect yourself by wearing a pair of long, heavy, fireproof grilling gloves or oven mitts that cover a good part of your arms. Also, have a few cloth pot holders on standby as well.

Apron

Sizzling food tends to spit and splatter a bit. A thoughtfully chosen apron—say, one that declares you as "Grill Sergeant" or maybe "Thrilla of the Grilla"—will not only establish you as the host or hostess with the most, but will protect you and your party duds. Of course, "Mr. Good Lookin' is Cookin'" and "Miss Behavin" aprons will also set a certain tone for your party, even if you're just grilling for two.

Spatula

A grilling spatula should have a long handle and wide blade for easily slipping beneath food. Also, a long, angled or bent handle will keep your hand and arm away from the heat.

Barbecue Fork

A barbecue fork with a long handle is great for getting between the bars of the grate to loosen stubborn food.

Tongs

It is useful to have two pairs of tongs. One pair of metal grilling tongs should be long and strong, allowing you to gently, firmly, and safely grasp food, moving and turning it as needed. The other heavy-duty pair should be used for picking up the hot grate and moving around hot coals if need be. BTW, make life easy on your hands and choose spring-loaded tongs for all your grilling needs.

Skewers

Kebabs are a grilling staple! Therefore, skewers are a must-have for every griller. They come in lots of shapes and sizes, including some that are rather artistic and sculptural, and are often designed for specific foods. To keep things simple, always have eight to twelve metal skewers on hand, along with a skewer holder to support several skewers above the heat at the same time. Flat or wide-bladed metal skewers, as opposed to long metal sticks, are particularly helpful in keeping food, such as tempeh, seitan, and some fruits and vegetables, in place as you turn them. Skewers with heat-resistant handles will also make life easier. A common and disposable alternative to metal skewers is bamboo or wooden skewers, which come in different sizes and should be soaked in water for at least 20 to 30 minutes before grilling, to prevent burning. Two-pronged skewers are especially useful for grilling delicate items such as tofu.

Basting Brushes

To slather on all those lively oils, marinades, and sauces, choose a basting brush with a long wooden handle and natural or silicone bristles. To get really fancy, use a bundle of herbs to baste or brush them on. Not only is this an eye-catching detail to your grilling show, it will add an extra zip to your food, and it's disposable for easy cleanup.

Aluminum Foil

Heavy-duty aluminum foil serves two main purposes on the grill. First, you can create packets of ingredients, such as seasoned vegetables, to grill for an instant meal or side dish. And, second, you can grill food on top of the aluminum foil, which will ensure nothing slips through the grate. As a bonus, aluminum foil also comes in handy for discarding used charcoal (see page 11).

Grill Basket

All hail the genius who invented the grill basket. Whether long-handled, drum-shaped, flat, open-topped, compartmentalized, or custom-made for kebabs and corn on the cob, grill baskets allow you to easily handle small or delicate pieces of food. One general, medium-size grill basket will suit most grillers' needs, but it never hurts to have a few different types at your beck and call.

Grilling Screen

A nonstick grilling screen sets on the grate and allows you to grill small or delicate pieces of food without having to worry about them slipping through the bars.

Brushes and Scrubbers

You can tell a lot about backyard hosts or hostesses by how clean their grill is. A sturdy wire grill brush with attached scraper and a tough grill scrubber will enable you to clean the grate and firebox completely, so it's ready to go for the next round of grilling adventures.

Chimney Starter

A chimney starter, made of metal and cylindrical in shape, really gives the eco-minded host or hostess the chance to put on a show for guests, while igniting charcoal to perfection and eliminating the need for lighter fluid. Crumpled sheets of newspaper are placed on the bottom below a wire partition and the charcoal goes on top. The newspaper is lit, and in 15 to 25 minutes, blazing coals are ready to do what they do best.

Electric Charcoal Starter

An electric charcoal starter is a simple device with a metal loop as the heating element attached to a handle. This tool is used by placing it between two layers of coal in the grill, plugging it in (using an outdoor extension cord if necessary), and waiting for a few minutes until the coals are glowing red. Using the handle, the device is then removed from the hot coals, unplugged, and left to cool on an appropriate, nonflammable surface.

Long-stemmed Lighter

This is the perfect lighter for igniting your chimney starter, self-lighting charcoal, outdoor candles and torches, or campfire, as the long stem will keep your hands out of harm's way. While these lighters are readily available in stores everywhere, Zippo's Outdoor Line of lighters is especially geared toward grilling and other outdoor activities (www.zippo.com).

Grill Cover

A sturdy weatherproof cover will protect your grill from the elements, and help maintain it for years to come. After all, remember that your grill is an investment in money, time, and fun, which is worth protecting. While grill covers are widely available, one go-to source with a large variety is The Cover Store (www.the-cover-store.com), which carries the CoverMates brand.

Grill Lights

Lights specifically designed for your grilling area are widely available and are invaluable when firing up after the sun goes down.

Fire Extinguisher

Hopefully you'll never need it, but a dry chemical fire extinguisher is nice to have nearby, just in case. To find the best one for your particular needs, check at your local hardware or outdoor store, or inquire at your local fire department about which extinguisher you should purchase.

Grill Pad or Patio Protector

This is an often-overlooked item that will go a long way in protecting the deck or patio surface beneath your grill. Fireproof grill pads are available from such sources as DiversiTech (www.grillingpad.com), or a heavy sheet of metal will also suffice.

Condiments Tray

Most larger grills have at least a small attached surface area where you can have easy access to utensils, seasonings, marinades, sauces, and other ingredients. To reduce the number of trips back inside for this or that, assemble everything you need for grilling on one designated tray and carry that outside to the grill. This will also make it easy to take everything back inside once the meal is over. While any type of tray will do, I prefer using a hand-wrought metal tray from Wendell August Forge (www.wendellaugust.com), which adds class and style to your *mise en place,* while becoming an instant heirloom to be handed down through the generations of grillers to come. These trays, which are available in many styles, also make perfect birthday, wedding, anniversary, hostess, and anytime gifts for those special grillers in your life.

Grill Towel

Grilling can get a little messy, which is par for the course. But instead of wasting paper towels, have a colorful cloth towel nearby for wiping off hands, making spills disappear, and easy cleanup. Golf towels are particularly good at pulling double duty as grill towels, hooks included.

Drip Pans

Aluminum foil drip pans ensure that any sauces or ingredients that try running away are caught and held as neatly as possible. Drip pans are also great for keeping food hot on the side while you finish preparing the meal, or while cooking with indirect heat (see page 10).

Spray Bottle

A spray bottle or mister is the perfect way to pamper your food with olive oil and other basting mixtures while they sizzle away on the grill. A spray bottle filled with water will also come in handy for any small flare-ups.

Mountain Pie Maker

Okay, so maybe technically this isn't an instrument of grilling, but (a) it's a close relative, and (b) there was no way I was writing this book and leaving it out. Inexpensive and readily available everywhere (www.pieiron.com is one go-to source), mountain pie makers consist of a heavy cast-iron shell that's perfect for holding two slices of bread with filling, and long steel handles with wooden grips. Whether you use apple, cherry, or some other sweet filling or create a mini pizza pocket, a mountain pie maker turns any campfire into a backwoods gourmet bonanza, especially when you want to impress your city friends. Check out the scrumptious homemade mountain pie recipes on pages 186–187, and find out for yourself. You can also find versions of mountain pie makers that are designed specifically to make burgers and other treats over a campfire.

Compost Bin

In addition to putting a satisfied smile on your face, the plant-based recipes in this book also let you give back to Mother Nature in a unique way. If you don't already have your own compost pile or bin, it's time to put the vegetable peelings, salad leaves, fruit scraps, and other biodegradable leftovers from these recipes to work in your garden to ensure you have even more fresh vegetables to grill in the future. For more information on composting, visit www.howtocompost.org.

Dinnerware for Outdoor Meals

Save money and add an extra touch of eco-style to your grilling dinner or blowout by setting your table with reusable dishes, glassware, silverware, and cloth napkins and tablecloths. At the very least, do Mother Nature a favor by using biodegradable and compostable dishes and napkins, or recycled-paper dinnerware and napkins along with unbleached paper cups. Check at your local grocery stores and online for these products.

SIZZLE FACTOR

When it comes to achieving the desired heat level on a grill, there are a few basic things every griller should know. One of the most important things to remember regarding the sizzle factor is that every grill is different, so regardless of what specific recipe instructions say about heat level and timing, it's always a good idea to stick close to the grill and carefully watch the food until it's done to your liking.

Direct Heat and Indirect Heat

When grilling, you will most often be dealing with what's called direct heat. This is when food is placed over the fire or heat source. Most of the food in this book, unless otherwise noted, will be cooked over direct heat at the appropriately noted temperature.

On a charcoal grill, this means positioning the food above an even layer of glowing coals, which are usually hot enough after 15 to 25 minutes. You can also create multiple heat zones by placing a majority of the hot coals to one side (such as two layers of coals), fewer coals next to that (such as a single layer), and then leave an empty zone for either indirect heating (discussion follows) or a safe haven for burning food to cool down. Some grills allow you to play around with heat levels by raising and lowering the grate.

On a gas grill, the food is placed over the hot burner(s) to utilize direct heat. Direct heat is easily achieved by preheating the grill to high for 10 to 15 minutes with the lid closed and then reducing the heat to medium, or according to the recipe directions for grilling. Just remember, *always* start a grill with the lid open.

When using direct heat, it's a good idea to leave at least one area of the charcoal grill or gas grill cool, either by not placing any coals there or by leaving a burner or two turned off. This way, should the food begin to burn, you will always have an escape route to cool it down quickly.

In addition to using direct heat, grillers also use indirect heat. Simply put, this means cooking food next to the fire or heat source, and not over it. On a charcoal grill, position the hot coals on both sides of the grill, using side baskets if you have them, while leaving the middle empty; or place all the charcoal on one half of the grill, leaving the other half empty; or a third option for a circular grill is to encircle the empty center with hot coals. Then, either place a drip pan in the middle and slow cook your food in there, or place the food on the grate over the empty zone. For a gas grill, leave a center burner or two off while igniting the burners around it. Preheat the outside burners on high for 10 to 15 minutes with the lid closed and then lower the heat to medium, or according to the recipe. Again, make sure the lid is initially up when you start the grill. Then cook the food over the unlit burner as directed.

Determining Heat Level
Charcoal Grill

Because charcoal grills don't have convenient knobs like gas grills for setting the heat level, you have to rely on good old-fashioned instinct, and touch. The following is the method that has been used by grillers for ages to make sure their charcoal or wood grill has reached the perfect sizzle factor.

Very carefully place your hand 3 to 4 inches above the grate and start counting by "one-thousands."

The length of time you can leave your hand over the grate will let you know the heat level:

- One to three one-thousand = High heat
- Four to five one-thousand = Medium-high heat
- Six to eight one-thousand = Medium heat
- Nine to ten one-thousand = Medium-low heat
- Eleven to thirteen one-thousand = Low heat

Charcoal grills usually hit the high heat mark after 15 to 25 minutes, when the charcoal is glowing and covered with a layer of gray ash, and they effectively burn for about an hour. If more coals need to be added, it's best to get them hot first in a chimney starter (see page 8) and then add them to the original coals.

To dispose of the coals when finished, let them cool completely (overnight is recommended), and then wrap them in aluminum foil and toss them in an outdoor trash can for regular pickup. In some cases, additive-free charcoal (crushed up) and ash can be used as fertilizer for some plants. Do your research to discover if charcoal and ash are appropriate for your particular plants and gardens.

Gas Grill and Electric Grill

Heat level on a gas grill or electric grill is usually a matter of turning a few knobs until the required sizzle factor is achieved. When using a gas grill, *always always always* open the lid before turning on the gas. It's a good idea to then preheat the grill, with the lid closed to keep in the heat, on high for about 10 minutes before cooking. When you're finished cooking, always remember to turn off the gas and the burners, or unplug an electric grill.

Be sure to read the manufacturer's instructions for using the heat controls on any grill, as each one is a little different.

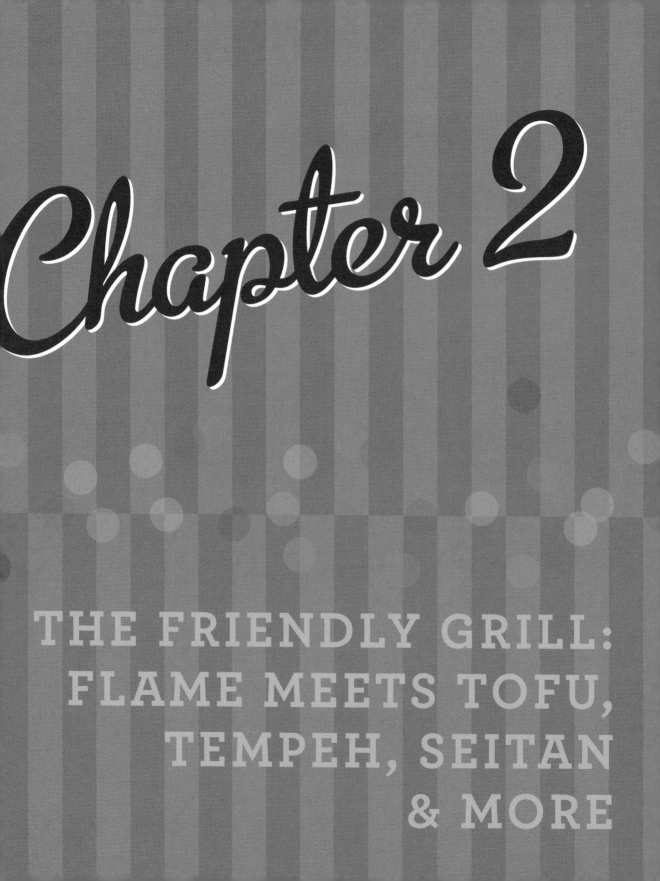

Chapter 2

THE FRIENDLY GRILL: FLAME MEETS TOFU, TEMPEH, SEITAN & MORE

Until now, grilling has almost exclusively been associated with meat. But grills across the planet are about to gain more friends and get more action than they ever could have dreamed of. Grilled vegetables have long garnered rave reviews, but now a new brigade of protein-packed tummy pleasers is also joining the festivities big time, and they're ready to turn your barbecue into a mouthwatering blast of flavor.

Tofu, tempeh, and seitan are expanding and, indeed, revolutionizing the way people eat, and now grill. With their extraordinary ability to easily absorb and assume the flavors of the same favorite marinades and sauces used for meat, and so much more, these three marvels convey a simple message to their meaty counterparts: "Anything you can do, we can do better!" In other words, so much more than packaged veggie burgers and chik'n strips can do a friendly grill proud. And while you may think you know all about this trifecta of vegan bliss, make sure to read the following for some grill-friendly tips and tricks.

My friends, meet the newest superstars of the grill and picnic table.

TOFU

A worldwide favorite for about two thousand years running, tofu, also known as bean curd, is a soy product made from pressing soy milk curds into blocks, which come in soft/silken and firm/extra-firm varieties. For grilling purposes, firm or extra-firm tofu is the best to use. High in protein, calcium, and iron, the beauty of tofu is its amazing versatility. Possessing little taste as is, tofu acts as a magical sponge, soaking up whatever flavors it is combined with, such as sweet or spicy seasonings and marinades. This talent for transforming itself into whatever the host or hostess desires is what makes tofu a welcomed guest at any party, especially grill fests.

One word of caution: Tofu loves the grill so much, it sometimes tends to be clingy, so be sure to oil the grate before using the grill, well marinate the tofu, and have a spatula or barbecue fork nearby for gently nudging it when needed.

Pressing and Draining Tofu

Before grilling tofu, you have to press and drain it to remove excess water. This will firm up the tofu even more, making the grilling process a little easier.

Cut the firm or extra-firm tofu block into desired pieces, usually bite size or ¾-inch slices. Cover a plate or slanted cutting board (with a catch pan at the bottom) with an absorbent dish towel or paper towels. Place a single layer of tofu pieces on the surface. Cover the tofu layer with another dish towel or paper towels. Top that layer with a heavy object, such as a plate with canned vegetables on top of it, a cutting board, or a weighty skillet. Allow the tofu to drain for at least 30 minutes to an hour.

If you have any extra tofu that will not be used immediately, do not press and drain it. Place it in a sealed container, cover with water, and refrigerate. Replace the water every day. Opened tofu keeps fresh for at least three to four days.

Freezing Tofu

Some people prefer to freeze tofu, for a chewier texture. Doing this also helps the tofu better absorb marinades and other seasonings. To freeze, first cut the tofu as desired and drain it as instructed, getting as much of the water out as possible. Leftover water will form ice pockets in the tofu, leaving holes when thawed. Then, either wrap the tofu in plastic wrap or place it in a resealable plastic bag, and store it in the freezer for up to 5 or 6 months. After only a few days, the frozen tofu will assume a chewy texture. To thaw, simply place the tofu in the refrigerator overnight.

Tofu has a tendency to take on a yellowish hue when frozen, but this is natural and nothing to worry about.

Here's a basic grilled tofu recipe that you can put your own twist on, especially if you've never grilled with it before:

Quick Grilled Tofu on Stilts

Because tofu at its firmest is still a soft ingredient, it often helps to secure each piece with two skewers (or a double-pronged skewer), which the Japanese refer to as tofu on stilts or *dengaku*.

For quick and easy Grilled Tofu on Stilts, after pressing and draining the tofu as noted, place the tofu in a marinade of choice (see Chapter 7 for a wide variety of great suggestions), cover, and let sit for 1 to 2 hours (the longer the better), turning over the tofu once halfway through the marinating time. Insert the presoaked bamboo skewers or metal skewers. Place the tofu on a medium to hot grill, or grilling screen, for 4 to 6 minutes per side, or

until golden. Continue to brush with the marinade while grilling.

Make sure your grate is well brushed and oiled before grilling the tofu. This will help ensure the tofu doesn't stick to the grate bars.

For more grilled tofu recipes, check out TLT on page 140, Halftime Pizza on page 144, Presto Pesto No-Bake Lasagne on page 165, Chipotle-Marinated Tofu & Vegetable Kebabs on page 172, and Zucchini, Squash & Mushroom Kebabs on page 173, as well as the marinades in Chapter 7.

TEMPEH

Like tofu, and originally hailing from Indonesia, tempeh (tem-pay) is a soybean-based product, or fermented soybean cake. Its utilization of the entire soybean and its fermentation process empower this treat with a power-punch of protein, vitamins, calcium, and dietary fiber. It has a firm texture and a nutty and mushroomlike, earthy flavor that make it a rock star among foodies, and especially nice for grilling. Tempeh comes in a wide range of varieties and flavors; the recipes in this book were tested with regular, unflavored soy tempeh, but you should feel free to experiment with other varieties and flavors.

Just like most rock stars, tempeh can be a little temperamental when it comes to performing, because it doesn't absorb flavors as swiftly as tofu or seitan does. The secret to winning over this little diva is to pamper it (a.k.a., simmer) in vegan vegetable broth or water for 10 to 15 minutes (to soften it and make it more absorbent for the marinade), drain, and then let it bask in the marinade a little longer.

Here's a basic grilled tempeh recipe that you can put your own twist on, especially if you've never grilled with it before:

Quick Grilled BBQ Tempeh

Slice and cut the tempeh as desired, such as into 1- or ½-inch-thick slices or bite-size pieces. Tempeh triangles are also nice for grilling. To create triangles, slice the tempeh cake in half, and then cut the two halves into four triangles.

If desired, simmer the tempeh in vegan vegetable broth or water for 10 to 15 minutes, then drain. Then, place the tempeh into a *flavorful* barbecue sauce (or marinade) of choice (see Chapter 7 for a wide variety of great suggestions), cover, and let sit for 2 to 3 hours to overnight (the longer the better, as it takes longer for tempeh to absorb flavors), turning the tempeh over once halfway through the marinating time. You can then either insert presoaked bamboo skewers or metal skewers, or use a grill basket or grilling screen.

Place the tempeh on a medium to hot grill for 4 to 6 minutes per side, or until browned. Continue to brush with the sauce or marinade while grilling.

Make sure your grate is well brushed and oiled before grilling the tempeh. This will help make sure the tempeh doesn't stick to the grate bars.

One further tempeh tip: After you're finished grilling the tempeh, remove it from the grill and let it sit for 2 to 3 minutes undisturbed, which will allow the grill marks to take hold.

For more grilled tempeh recipes, check out Grilled Tempeh Satay on page 43, Maple-Soy Tempeh over Rice on page 168, Tex-Mex Tempeh for Two on page 170, and Tempeh Steaks on the Grill on page 171, as well as the marinades in Chapter 7.

SEITAN

Seitan (say-tan) is made from the gluten of wheat. Wheat flour dough is washed with water to dissolve the starch, leaving only the elastic gluten, which is high in protein. For anyone who still has a hankering for meat, seitan is particularly known for its ability to take on the texture and flavor of meat. In fact, some varieties of seitan are flavored to taste like chicken, beef, or other meats. In this book, when seitan is used, it is the regular, unflavored seitan, but as with tempeh, by all means, feel free to experiment. Because seitan sometimes tends to crumble or break into small pieces, a grill pan or grilling screen will be a trusted wingman with this delicacy.

Here's a basic grilled seitan recipe that you can put your own twist on, especially if you've never grilled with it before:

Quick Grilled Hot "Wing" Seitan

When grilled, seitan becomes crispy on the outside while remaining tender on the inside. To make a basic hot "wing" version of seitan, cut the seitan into bite-size pieces or leave as a larger piece, depending on preference. Place the seitan in a *flavorful* hot sauce (or marinade) of choice (see Chapter 7 for a wide variety of great suggestions), cover, and let sit for 1 to 2 hours (the longer the better), turning the seitan over once halfway through the marinating time.

Then, for smaller, bite-size pieces, either secure them on skewers to grill, or place them in a grill basket or on a grilling screen. A larger piece of seitan can be placed directly on a hot grill or grilling screen.

Grill over medium to high heat for 6 to 8 minutes per side for the larger piece, or turn the smaller pieces on the skewers or in the basket every 2 minutes for 6 to 8 minutes, or until browned and crispy. Continue to brush with the sauce or marinade while grilling.

Bite-size vegetables, such as red bell peppers, onions, broccoli, eggplant, zucchini or summer squash, mushrooms, and cherry tomatoes, can also be added to the skewers. (Of course, cool celery sticks on the side are also a simple and nice counterpoint to the hot seitan "wings.")

Make sure your grate is well brushed and oiled before grilling the seitan. This will help make sure the seitan doesn't stick to the grate bars, if you're preparing it directly on them.

For more grilled seitan recipes, check out Golden Tandoori Seitan on page 34 and Seitan Flares on page 150, as well as the marinades in Chapter 7.

Note: To achieve the grill's trademark cross-hatch pattern on flat pieces of tofu, tempeh, or seitan (or any other item), when grill marks appear about halfway through the cooking time on each side, rotate the item 45 degrees and grill for the remainder of the time on that side.

VEGAN BURGERS

Not all store-bought veggie burgers are created equal. While the most popular brands, such as Boca (www.bocaburger.com), Morningstar Farms (www.morningstarfarms.com), Gardenburger (www.gardenburger.com), and Gardein (www.gardein.com), offer a variety of different types, some are vegetarian and others are vegan. You have to do your homework and visit each brand's Web site to discern between vegetarian and vegan burgers, and then make your choice. Taste is also a matter of personal preference, as veggie burgers come in a variety of flavors, based on their ingredients.

For last-minute or really lazy day meals, store-bought veggie burgers are a snap to toss on the grill, and they work well with all your favorite toppings—ketchup, mustard, onions, lettuce/spinach, tomatoes, and salsa (see Salsa Grand Slam on page 148). Always follow the cooking directions on the package. If no directions are given for grilling, grill the burgers over medium heat for several minutes, turning at least once or twice, until heated all the way through, 8 to 10 minutes, depending on the thickness of the patty.

The same is true for the meatless chik'n products sold by the aforementioned companies. They can be tossed on the grill and in minutes you have an instant entrée. Chik'n products can especially be dressed up with buffalo wing sauce or a favorite hot sauce (see Drop It like It's Hot Sauce on page 118 or the sauce used for Seitan Flares on page 150) and spicy salsa.

Packaged veggie burgers aside, a burger renaissance is sweeping the globe, inspiring handcrafted veggie burgers of all kinds. Vegans and vegetarians no longer will get the short end of the grill, as it were, having to rely solely on processed burgers from the freezer. Making veggie burgers at home and tossing them on the grill is easy and yields much tastier results. To make your own veggie burgers, which takes a little extra effort but is well worth it, check out the selection in Chapter 8, which includes Slip-N-Sliders, Stacked Portobello Burgers, Garbanzo & Herb Burgers with Creamy Lemon Tahini Sauce, Mexican Tortilla Burgers, Southwestern Burgers with Salsa, and Italian Herb Burgers on Focaccia, as well as a collection of other grilled sandwiches.

VEGAN HOT DOGS & SAUSAGES

Vegan hot dogs and sausages from such companies as Tofurky (www.tofurky.com) and Lightlife (www.lightlife.com) let you have a wiener roast just like anyone else. But again, check to make sure you're getting exactly what you want, as some varieties are vegetarian and some are vegan. And always follow the cooking directions on the package. If no grilling directions are given, grill the hot dogs and sausages over medium heat, while periodically turning them, until heated through, 8 to 10 minutes, depending on the consistency and desired doneness.

Much like their meaty counterparts, many packaged vegan hot dogs and sausages are high in sodium and filled with preservatives. So be sure to read labels and choose the best option for you. But also consider making your own. The Internet offers a variety of interesting recipes you can experiment with, and books such as *Vegan Brunch* by Isa Chandra Moskowitz provide inspired takes on homemade sausages you may have thought you'd never get to enjoy again.

VEGETABLES

You can literally grill a garden of vegetables. In fact, veggies and grills are very much a match made in foodie heaven!

Asparagus, eggplant, red bell peppers, onions, corn on the cob, mushrooms, zucchini, cauliflower—the list goes on and on. Whether arranged on a skewer, sliced and grilled directly, or seasoned and wrapped in an aluminum foil packet, grilling vegetables over medium heat is about as easy as it gets. And if you add marinated tofu, tempeh, and seitan to the mix, the sky is the limit.

To quickly and easily grill veggies, cut your favorite vegetables in similarly sized pieces for even grilling and brush them with extra-virgin olive oil or a favorite marinade; season to taste with salt, pepper, and whatever else you'd like; and let them meet their fiery maker, until tender or done as desired. Brushing with olive oil also ensures they won't stick to the grate. For smaller and slender vegetables or the more delicate variety, you may want to use a grilling screen or grill basket so they don't fall through the grate.

You'll find a majority of the recipes that follow throughout this book take advantage of this unique love affair between vegetable and grill, allowing you and your guests to further enjoy grilling in all its glory.

When it comes to grilling vegetables, most often their delicate flavors need only a few moments on a grill over direct heat to transform, bloom, and ultimately stand on their own as a side dish or snack. It's important to not leave vegetables lingering on the grill for too long, or else the charred smokiness and direct heat can overpower them—although a little charring, such as on broccoli and asparagus, is always welcome in my book. Indirect heat works well for simply warming vegetables and for maintaining more control, especially if you are new to grilling.

Ultimately, grilled vegetable dishes are all about balance. This is often achieved by pairing, or more aptly, layering, grilled vegetables with nongrilled vegetables and other foods and seasonings that will all complement each other. For example, the Pasta Salad with Grilled Summer Vegetables on page 64 takes a classic picnic dish and interjects grilled smokiness into the mix. This dish is successful because the neutral fusilli or gemelli provides a stunning foundation for evenly distributing

the burst of grilled flavors provided by the zucchini, green onions, bell peppers, and tomatoes, which even among themselves range from subtle to acidic. The overall taste is then further complemented and enhanced by the garlicky olive oil and red wine vinegar marinade, and seasonings such as oregano and basil. For the Romaine Holiday on page 52, grilling softens the bitter romaine just enough to play host to the lightly toasted sunflower seeds and pine nuts sprinkled on top, and the drizzling of balsamic vinegar.

This concept of grilling and layering greens may be new to you, but it will rock your world once you understand how easy it is. You could say the whole thing is literally a matter of taste. If you think about it, our palate is naturally set to seek out this balance of different flavors. In fact, we innately know a recipe has struck this harmony of flavors because those are the dishes we instantly declare as delicious. Each vegetable and the accompanying ingredients in the recipes that follow play their part in contributing to the greater and seamless *ah-ha* moment of every bite. This is the ying and yang of grilling to perfection.

For more information about grilling various vegetables beyond the recipes in this book, refer to the "Grilling Times for Fruits and Vegetables" chart at http://grillingtips.com.

FRUIT

You may not think of fruit and grill as a likely match, but think again! Like vegetables, fruits also have a special affinity for grills. During summer especially, grilled fruit works in a multitude of combinations, such as for simple, light, and satisfying desserts when more time-consuming options are out of the question.

Heavier fruits such as pineapples work well on grills, as in Grilled Pineapple Rings with Sorbet on page 189; whereas softer fruits, such as peaches, need extra attention or else they can become mushy, but with skins left on and a little tender care, they are well worth it (e.g., Party on South Peach Salsa on page 42 and Grilled Peaches with Raspberry Sauce on page 180). Also, because fruit is loaded with water, it tends to get very hot on the grill, so be careful to let it cool a bit before eating.

As opposed to normally hearty vegetables, fruit is often grilled over indirect heat, or once the coals begin to burn down. For the recipes here, particularly the desserts in Chapter 11, direct heat is used, but if you're new to grilling and want to take things a bit slower, feel free to start with indirect heat and work your way to direct heat. The most important thing is to stick close to the grill and watch the fruit, ensuring that it grills just how you want it.

If you want to experiment with grilling different types of fruit, just be sure that the fruit won't stick to the grates. A light coating of canola or vegetable oil will usually prevent sticking. Also, using a grilling screen, grill basket, or skewers will help keep your fruit above board.

Much like with vegetables, pairing a selection of complementary fruit and seasonings or sauces is always a crowd-pleaser. For example, the Fruity Kebabs Brushed with Brown Sugar, Cinnamon & Mint on page 179 combine a range of fruit flavors such as apples, bananas, peaches, kiwis, pineapple, and strawberries to temper a cloyingly sweet result. This flavor combo is further balanced with a brown sugar, cinnamon, and mint mixture. Even simpler, the Tattooed Watermelon Salad on page 61 takes summer's juiciest fruit and lightly flames it, which adds an unexpected hint of smokiness that works nicely when the grilled watermelon slice is then placed atop arugula tossed in balsamic vinegar. And with a sprinkling of smoked salt, yet one more layer of flavor is added to the fruit's normally gentle profile, taking the dish in a sophisticated direction while still managing to remain as casual as you want it to be.

For more information about grilling various fruits beyond the recipes in this book, refer to the "Grilling Times for Fruits and Vegetables" chart at http://grillingtips.com.

THE FRIENDLY GRILL PANTRY

It would be impossible to always have every ingredient on hand, but it is certainly helpful to have a pantry of basics close by for whenever the grill calls. The following list lays out many of the standard ingredients that are either used frequently throughout the book in various recipes or that have a starring role in a dish that you will likely return to on a regular basis. These are ingredients that you will use throughout your cooking, but they will particularly shine at grill time.

Please note that several ingredients throughout the book have been denoted as "vegan" (e.g., vegan bread, vegan Dijon mustard, vegan salsa). At its most basic, this denotation means that you should pay extra attention when buying these products and carefully read their ingredient label to determine if they are indeed animal free (such as free of casein or lactose; if the ingredient label lists "plant-derived-lactose," however, that is fine). It does not mean that you have to seek a brand that specifically labels the item as "vegan."

Alcohol

Every attempt has been made to confirm that the alcohol used throughout this book is either inherently vegan or produced in vegan forms by various brands. For more information on vegan brands of alcohol, please visit www.barnivore.com.

The alcohol used in this book, both in a few of the food recipes and for the cocktail recipes in Chapter 12, includes:

- amaretto
- apricot liqueur
- beer, lager of choice
- bitters, Angostura
- brandy
- bourbon
- champagne
- cognac
- gin
- orange liqueur, including Cointreau, triple sec, and blue curaçao
- red wine, dry
- rice wine
- rum, including white rum, coconut-flavored rum, gold rum, dark rum, and light rum
- schnapps, including peach schnapps, peppermint schnapps, and strawberry schnapps
- sherry
- sloe gin
- Southern Comfort
- strawberry liqueur
- tawny or port wine
- tequila
- vermouth
- vodka, vanilla- and blueberry-flavored vodka
- white wine, dry

Beans

Beans are a vegan's best friend; well, one of them, anyway. It's always nice to have a variety of beans in the pantry. For our grilling purposes here, a supply of garbanzo beans, black beans, and kidney beans will suffice.

Bread

A variety of different breads are used throughout this book, such as thick bread for the Halftime Pizza on page 144, French or Italian bread for the Summer Bruschettas on page 37, potato bread rolls for the Stacked Portobello Burgers on page 123, sourdough bread for The Blue Pear on page 133, and regular sandwich bread for a variety of other recipes, including the homemade croutons on page 58. Regarding the bread used in the recipes, just as for all products, when shopping read the ingredient labels carefully to determine if a certain brand of bread is vegan, or visit the brand's Web site. Sometimes, bread will contain sugar, milk, butter, or honey. You can also find many homemade vegan bread recipes online. For the recipes that follow, feel free to experiment with different bread types, including making your own, while still sticking close to the recipe.

Cheese, Vegan

Vegan cheese is pretty widely available, but if you can't find it, it is available online at such sites as www.cosmosveganshoppe.com. Don't just trust the term *nondairy*; read labels carefully for the word *vegan*, watching out for soy- or rice-based brands that still list casein, which is milk protein, as an ingredient. Unfortunately, not all vegan cheese is created the same, taste-wise. Some reliable brands of vegan cheese are available from www.buteisland.com and www.daiyafoods.com. Also, be sure

to check out the Homemade Vegan Parmesan Cheese recipe on page 166.

Vegan cream cheese, which is used both for the Veggie Quesadillas with Sparky Corn Relish on page 162 and Zucchinicotti on page 166, is becoming more widely available in grocery stores and can also be purchased online at www.tofutti.com or www.followyourheart.com.

Chocolate, Vegan

Vegan chocolate is available from such online sites as www.veganessentials.com. In stores, read the ingredient label carefully to determine whether the chocolate contains any dairy products; ideally, it has been manufactured in a dedicated dairy-free environment. Here, it is used to make S'More Is Always Better! on page 185 and Chocolate-Dipped Coconut Islands on page 183. Also, Santa Cruz Organic Chocolate Syrup (www.scojuice.com) is great for dipping or drizzling on fruit, such as the coconut islands, strawberries, bananas, and so much more, and is even available in different flavors. Let's face it, there's always a reason to have chocolate around!

Extra-Virgin Olive Oil

Extra-virgin olive oil may be the single most used ingredient in this book, so you may want to have an extra bottle on hand in addition to the one you're using. Just about everything benefits from a brushing of olive oil before hitting the grill, including the grill grate itself. Extra-virgin olive oil is the most flavorful and highest quality of the olive oils. Moreover, it's made without using chemicals. Olive oils can range in price widely, but for grilling, a less expensive, moderately priced extra-virgin olive oil is fine.

For more information on all things olive oil, go to www.oliveoilsource.com.

Other oils used in the book include canola oil, vegetable oil, toasted sesame oil, and truffle oil.

Fruit

The best fruit is always that which is in season and fresh from a local fruit stand or farmers' market, or picked by you. The following is a list of the fruits that are used frequently throughout this book and/or which are the subject of their own recipe:

- apples (fruit and juice)
- avocados
- bananas
- cantaloupes
- cherries
- coconuts
- kiwis
- lemons (juice and zest)
- limes (juice and zest)
- oranges (juice and zest; mandarin oranges)
- papaya
- peaches
- pears
- pineapple (fruit and juice)
- raspberries
- strawberries
- watermelon

Herbs and Spices

Herbs and spices really do make the world go around. A pinch of this herb or of that spice can completely revive, refresh, and transform a dish right before your eyes. A well-stocked spice rack is an ever-evolving thing, but it will come in just as handy for grilling as for any other cooking. Herbs and spices play nicely with the grill to raise the flavor profile of fruits, vegetables, and meat analogues such as tofu, tempeh, and seitan. They can also be fun to experiment with when trying to switch up a dish.

The herbs and spices used most in this book include:

HERBS:
- basil
- chervil
- cilantro
- dill
- marjoram
- mint
- oregano
- parsley
- rosemary
- sage
- savory
- tarragon
- thyme

SPICES:
- allspice
- caraway seeds
- cardamom
- cayenne pepper
- chile powder
- cinnamon
- cloves
- coriander
- cumin
- garam masala (also see the homemade version on page 35)
- garlic powder
- ginger
- mace
- mustard seeds (yellow)
- nutmeg
- onion powder
- paprika (Hungarian if you can find it)
- pepper (black and white)
- pickling spice
- red pepper flakes
- salt (regular, sea, seasoned, and smoked)
- turmeric

Hot Sauce

A few of the recipes, such as the Mexican Tortilla Burgers on page 125, Seitan Flares on page 150, and Salsa Grand Slam on page 148, call for a hot sauce of choice. While Tabasco sauce will always be the original liquid fire, one of the quintessential go-to hot sauces is Frank's Red Hot Cayenne Pepper Sauce (www.franksredhot.com).

Margarine, Vegan

Where a recipe calls for "vegan margarine" as a substitute for traditional butter, I suggest using the Earth Balance brand of buttery spreads (www.earthbalancenatural.com) or another trans fat-free, nonhydrogenated vegan margarine of choice.

Marshmallows, Vegan

Vegan marshmallows, which don't contain gelatin, are available from such sources as www.sweetandsara.com, as well as various kosher brands that also omit the gelatin. Although they are only used for one recipe in this book, S'More Is Always Better! on page 185, they are something you will *always* want to have on hand, just like the vegan graham crackers that are also available from the same Web site. Even if you're not making s'mores, these vegan marshmallows are also great for toasting over a campfire and eating them solo, as they react to flame in the same way as traditional marshmallows do.

Mayonnaise, Vegan

When store-bought vegan mayonnaise is called for, Vegenaise is the recommended brand. Vegenaise is becoming more widely available in stores, but can also be purchased online at www.followyourheart.com, which is the company that originally created it. For homemade vegan mayo, check out pages 77 and 156 for two different versions that can be used throughout this book.

Milk, Vegan

Vegan (nondairy) milk is widely available in grocery stores. Recipes here call for regular and vanilla-flavored soy milk, but rice or almond milk will also work.

Mustard, Vegan

Many of the recipes herein specify "vegan" Dijon mustard, which means, as always, read the ingredient label of any mustard you're buying to ensure you are getting exactly what you want. Some Dijon mustards contain egg or lactose, for example. You cannot take for granted that something as seemingly innocuous as mustard will always be vegan.

Nutritional Yeast

Also called "nooch," nutritional yeast is a mustard-colored yeast that is heralded for its cheesy and even nutty flavor. Available in flakes or powder form, it's especially effective in place of cheese in many dishes. For example, nutritional yeast adds a nice accent when used for Skinny Dipping Taters on page 39, Grill-Baked Potatoes on page 97, Grilled Picnic Pizza on page 167, or when making the Homemade Vegan Parmesan Cheese on page 166. Just to be clear, it's not brewer's yeast or any other kind of yeast. It's found in most health food stores and online.

Seitan

See page 17.

Sour Cream and Yogurt, Vegan

Vegan sour cream, such as Tofutti Sour Supreme, is available online at such sites as www.tofutti.com; www.followyourheart.com also produces a tasty sour cream alternative. Or, see the homemade vegan version on page 39. Also, use plain (unflavored, unsweetened) vegan soy yogurt when it is called for; read the label carefully to ensure it is completely dairy free. Vegan sour cream and plain vegan yogurt can be used interchangeably, if necessary.

Soy Sauce

Wherever soy sauce is used throughout the book, a low-sodium version can be substituted if desired. Read the label carefully to ensure it does not contain lactic acid. Also, Bragg Liquid Aminos is a natural, soybean-based alternative to traditional soy sauce that is gaining momentum. Check it out at www.bragg.com.

Sugar, Vegan

Regular white, refined table sugar is often made using animal bone char and is thus avoided by vegans. Therefore, where you see "sugar" used herein, you can use vegan granulated sugars, such as the Florida Crystals brand (www.floridacrystals.com), or other vegan sugar substitutes of choice.

Tahini

Tahini, a paste made from ground sesame seeds, is a staple in any vegan pantry. Often used in hummus dishes, here it pulls double duty in Garbanzo & Herb Burgers with Creamy Lemon Tahini Sauce on page 126, appearing in both the burger and sauce recipes.

Tempeh

See page 16.

Tofu

Soft/silken and firm/extra-firm varieties of tofu are used throughout the book. For more information, please see page 14.

Vegetable Broth, Vegan

While most store-bought vegetable broths will be vegan, and will be usable for many of your recipes, both in this book and in your other cooking, always read the ingredients on the labels of prepared foods and broths to make certain that the brand you're buying is, indeed, completely animal free. A few brands to consider using are Rapunzel Organics Vegan Vegetable Bouillon (www.internatural-foods.com), Trader Joe's Savory Broth—Vegetable (www.traderjoes.com), and Vogue Cuisine Instant VegeBase (www.voguecuisine.com).

Vegetables

The best vegetables are always those that are in season and fresh from a local vegetable stand or farmers' market, or from your own garden. The following is a list of the vegetables that are most used throughout this book and/or which are the subject of their own recipe:

- artichokes
- arugula
- asparagus
- bell peppers (red, yellow, and green)
- broccoli
- carrots
- cauliflower

- chives
- corn on the cob
- cucumber
- edamame
- eggplants (Japanese, white, and common purple variety, if not otherwise noted)
- garlic
- green onions and scallions
- jalapeños (including chipotles)
- kale
- leeks
- lettuce (various kinds, such as radicchio, romaine, and Bibb)
- mushrooms (various kinds; mostly portobello)
- okra
- onions (various kinds, such as sweet, red, and green)
- poblano peppers
- potatoes (various kinds, such as baking potatoes, russet, Yukon Gold, and baby red or white)
- sweet potatoes
- tomatoes (various kinds, such as cherry, plum, pear, and sun-dried)
- shallots
- shishito peppers
- spinach
- squash (yellow, summer, and spaghetti)
- string beans
- Swiss chard
- zucchini

Vinegars

Vinegars add zest to many dishes in this book and can range in flavors and uses. When part of a marinade, vinegar gives a noticeable jolt of energy to grilled vegetables, fruit, and meat analogues. Here, the most used varieties are balsamic, apple cider, malt, and red wine.

Worcestershire Sauce, Vegan

Traditional Worcestershire sauce is made using anchovies, and therefore not vegan. Luckily for a number of marinades and other dishes, vegan Worcestershire sauce is becoming more widely available in stores. Also, see the homemade vegan version on page 108. Here, it is used in such marinades as Finger-Lickin' BBQ Sauce on page 108, Pineapple Does the Teriyaki on page 110, Apple Cider Harvest on page 111, and Get Tangy with It on page 115.

Chapter 3

BACKYARD BITES

There's something about fresh air, sunshine, and the distinct aroma of a fired-up grill that teases the appetite and leaves all of us searching for a sizzling snack to nibble on. While your house may be your castle, the backyard is your kingdom, and there your grill is standing ever ready to serve you.

No longer will you be stuck in the kitchen while all your guests, whether only a few or many, many more, are having fun out back without you. Now with a few simple and fresh ingredients, you can turn the grill into a hub of activity while you prepare and serve up wave after wave of these quick and easy light bites.

For your next get-together, be it a family picnic or swanky bonfire of the vanities, leave it to your grill to whip out these appetizers in no time, and in batches that can easily be doubled or tripled to get the party started. Grill-amped classics such as bruschetta, loaded potato skins, peach salsa, eggplant rounds, and even seasoned popcorn join several new "grate" stars such as shishito peppers, edamame, tandoori seitan, minty pesto triangles, and artichokes, guaranteeing your guests won't be able to keep their hands off the finger foods.

Or, should you decide to take your grill on a road trip, these dishes also work well when served around a campfire or for entertaining RV style.

1 cup (or more) shishito peppers

2 teaspoons canola or extra-virgin olive oil

Sea salt

Cayenne pepper (optional)

Shishito Heat Wave

What could easily be the love child of a bell pepper and a jalapeño, these mild-flavored shishito peppers are the newest dazzlers on the grilling circuit. About one in ten are very hot, while the rest are mildly spicy. Packed with vitamins A and C, shishitos are a popular treat in Japan, but are also becoming more widely available in grocery stores everywhere. However, if you can't find shishitos, use poblanos instead. A platter of these showstoppers at the beginning of a party won't stick around for long, but your guests sure will.

Heat a grill pan over medium heat until hot but not smoking, or heat the grill to medium.

In a bowl, coat the peppers with the canola oil. Place the peppers either in the grill pan or on a grilling screen (they can also be skewered for this, if desired). Grill the peppers, shaking the grill pan or turning them on the grilling screen until they are blistered and puffed up, even charred in places, but not burned, 1 to 2 minutes. When the peppers begin to deflate, pour them onto a paper towel-lined plate. Sprinkle with the sea salt and serve immediately. For an extra kick, also sprinkle with the cayenne.

YIELD: 2 servings

1 large red onion

½ cup tomato sauce

½ cup vegan soy yogurt

1 teaspoon chopped fresh ginger

2 cloves garlic, peeled

1 to 2 jalapeños, stemmed and seeded (if desired—the heat is mostly in the inside ribs)

¼ teaspoon cayenne pepper, or more to taste

½ teaspoon cumin or (preferably) toasted cumin seeds (see toasting directions)

1 teaspoon garam masala (see note) (store-bought, or see recipe that follows)

¼ teaspoon ground cloves

½ teaspoon turmeric

½ teaspoon salt

½ teaspoon freshly ground black pepper

1 pound seitan, sliced into large chunks

Note: Garam masala, which is an Indian blend of spices, is becoming more widely available in supermarkets, but it's also available online at www.kalustyans.com. Also see the homemade version, which follows.

Golden Tandoori Seitan

There's nothing quite like slow-cooked Indian food from a tandoor clay oven, which is among the hottest ovens in the world. This seitan dish uses an electrifying blend of spices and soy yogurt for a homemade version to be grilled outdoors.

In a blender or food processor, process all the ingredients, except the seitan, until smooth. Transfer the mixture to a bowl and add the seitan. Stir gently to coat the seitan thoroughly.

Heat the grill to medium-high.

Skewer the seitan pieces and grill until browned, 6 to 8 minutes, basting with any leftover sauce.

YIELD: 4 to 6 servings

Note: As in any skewer recipe, if you're using bamboo or wooden skewers, soak them in water for at least 20 to 30 minutes before threading on the food, to avoid burning the skewers.

To toast cumin seeds: In a dry skillet, toast the cumin seeds over medium heat (stovetop or gas or electric grill), shaking every 15 seconds, until the seeds just begin to smoke; then immediately transfer them to a bowl. Be careful, because cumin seeds can burn very easily.

garam masala

To maximize the complex flavors in this spice mixture, lightly toast the whole spices in a dry cast-iron skillet over medium heat, shaking the skillet every minute or so, until the spices are very fragrant, 3 to 4 minutes. Then grind the whole spices in an electric spice grinder (see note).

Place all the ingredients in a jar. Put the lid on the jar and shake the jar well to combine the spices. Store in a dry, cool place.

YIELD: About ¼ cup

1 tablespoon ground cumin

2 teaspoons ground coriander

2 teaspoons ground cardamom

1 teaspoon ground black pepper

1 teaspoon ground cinnamon

½ teaspoon ground cloves

½ teaspoon ground nutmeg

Note: For the homemade garam marsala, use an electric coffee grinder that you have designated for spices only, not one used for coffee.

Summer Bruschettas

It's time to slip on those Wayfarers, mellow out, and catch some rays with hunky, grilled bread that will turn heads, while the optional port wine adds a lightly sweet background to the balsamic and tomato mixture on top.

Heat the grill to medium-high.

In a large colander set over a bowl or in the sink, toss the tomatoes with the kosher salt and drain for 30 minutes.

On the grill, toast the bread slices on both sides. Rub the toasted top of each slice all over with the split garlic cloves and lightly brush the top of each slice with the olive oil.

Gently press down on the drained tomatoes to extract even more juices, transfer them to another bowl, and toss with the balsamic vinegar, wine, basil, oregano, and capers. Season to taste with the pepper. Spoon the tomato mixture in small mounds on top of the toasts and serve at once.

YIELD: 12 slices

4 medium-size tomatoes, peeled, seeded, and chopped very coarsely

2 teaspoons kosher salt

12 slices crusty vegan French or Italian bread, about 3 inches in diameter

3 cloves garlic, peeled and split

3 tablespoons extra-virgin olive oil

2 teaspoons balsamic vinegar

2 tablespoons tawny or ruby port wine (optional)

1 tablespoon thinly sliced fresh basil leaves

1 teaspoon dried oregano

1 tablespoon capers, drained well and rinsed, or more to taste

Freshly ground black pepper

2 shiny, firm eggplants, about
9 by 4 inches

Salt, as needed

Extra-virgin olive oil

A dry herb mixture of choice,
such as Italian

2 cups good tomato sauce, warmed

Grilled Eggplant & Herb Rounds with Tomato Sauce

Not only do people who say they don't like eggplant tend to devour this saucy snack, they're the first to fall in love with it, and to come back for seconds and thirds. A close relative of the tomato and potato, the eggplant takes nicely to the grill and easily absorbs the flavors of accompanying herbs and spices. Instead of rounds, eggplant can also be cut into small squares, oiled, skewered, and placed on the grill for 10 to 15 minutes, or until tender, for an easy appetizer or side dish.

Heat the grill to medium-high.

Cut the eggplant crosswise into ¼-inch slices. Salt the slices lightly on both sides and spread them out on paper towels. Let them stand and drain for 30 minutes, then pat dry.

Arrange the slices on cookie sheets or a grilling screen, paint them lightly with the olive oil, and sprinkle with the herbs. Grill for about 5 minutes on each side, or until just tender, but do not overcook—the slices should hold their shape.

Meanwhile, in a small saucepan, warm the tomato sauce. This can be done by placing the pan on the grill.

When the eggplant slices are tender, spread on each a generous spoonful of the tomato sauce. Dribble on droplets of olive oil. Serve at once.

YIELD: About 24 slices, serving 6 to 8

Skinny Dipping Taters

These potato skins, which are fully loaded with a horseradish mixture, green onions, tomatoes, and nooch, are as salubrious as they are delicious. Most of the nutrients in potatoes are in the skins, and the homemade sour cream used here is a much more inspired choice than its dairy doppelgänger.

Heat the oven to 350°F. Bake the potatoes for 1 hour. Let them cool for several minutes, then slice them in half lengthwise. Scoop out the potato flesh, leaving about ¼ inch of potato in the skins.

Heat the grill to medium. Brush the potatoes all over with the olive oil and season them with the salt and pepper. Place them on the grill and cook for about 10 minutes, or until crisp.

Meanwhile, in a small bowl, combine the sour cream with the horseradish, stirring well. When the potatoes are crisp, place them on four serving plates, fill them with the sour cream mixture, and sprinkle with the green onions, tomatoes, and nutritional yeast, if desired. Serve promptly.

YIELD: 4 servings

homemade vegan sour cream

In a standing blender, combine all the ingredients and blend for 5 minutes, until creamy and very smooth. Refrigerate for an hour or more to thicken. Keeps for about a week.

YIELD: 1½ cups

---

2 large russet potatoes, scrubbed clean

4 tablespoons extra-virgin olive oil

Salt and freshly ground black pepper

1 cup vegan sour cream (store-bought [page 27], or see recipe that follows) or plain vegan soy yogurt

2 tablespoons prepared horseradish, or to taste

4 green onions, white and light green parts only, trimmed and chopped finely

½ cup diced tomatoes, drained

Nutritional yeast, for sprinkling (optional)

HOMEMADE VEGAN SOUR CREAM

5 (1-inch) slices silken soft tofu, pressed and drained (see page 14)

1 tablespoon canola oil

4 teaspoons freshly squeezed lemon juice

2 teaspoons cider vinegar

1 teaspoon sugar

Salt and white pepper

1 (12-ounce) package frozen edamame, in the pods, thawed, or fresh edamame pods

2 tablespoons extra-virgin olive oil

Sea salt or kosher salt

Edamame Embers

Wholesome and enticing, edamame have enjoyed a tremendous upswing in popularity across the globe, and rightly so. This charred version of fresh soybeans will easily transition from a casual picnic with friends to a barefoot cocktail party under the stars. If necessary, remind your guests that the pods are inedible; they should gently suck the edamame beans from the pods using their mouth, then discard the pods.

In a medium-size bowl, toss the edamame in the olive oil. If using fresh edamame, boil them in water for 5 to 6 minutes and then toss in the olive oil before grilling.

In a grill basket, grill the edamame, tossing occasionally, for 4 to 5 minutes, or just until lightly browned. Season well with the sea salt.

YIELD: 6 appetizer servings, 3 side dish servings

4 medium-size ripe peaches, pitted and quartered, skin intact

Extra-virgin olive oil, for brushing the peaches

1 jalapeño, seeded and diced finely

1 small red onion, diced

Crushed red pepper (the more, the spicier!)

Salt and pepper

Juice of 1 lime, or to taste

Party on South Peach Salsa

Soft, juicy peaches may seem delicate but with a little tender loving care, they prove opposites do attract when they meet a flame head on. One secret is to not remove the skins, which helps the peaches stay intact and firm, but be sure to remove the pits. And when you throw jalapeño, onion, and crushed red pepper into the mix for this salsa, the summit of sweet and hot accents will win over any crowd!

Heat the grill to medium.

Brush the quartered peaches with the olive oil. Grill the peaches until nicely charred (or browned as desired), 3 to 5 minutes per side. Removing the skin is optional after grilling. Dice the peaches.

In a medium-size bowl, combine the peaches with the rest of the ingredients, mixing well. The salsa can be served warm or after being refrigerated to let the flavors further set.

Serve with tortilla chips, or as a tantalizing garnish for your favorite dish.

YIELD: About 3 cups, serving 4 to 6

Grilled Tempeh Satay
with Peach Dipping Sauce

Grills easily double as all-access passports for back-yard foodies, allowing adventurous palates to travel the world without ever having to leave the comfort of home. Here, you and your guests will embark on an excursion to Indonesia where grilled tempeh skewers are popular street food snacks. The peach dipping sauce further infuses the dish with bursts of international pizzazz.

Heat the grill to medium-high.

Make the satay skewers: In a blender, combine the shallot, lemongrass, ginger, and garlic. Blend until finely chopped. Add the coconut milk, chili sauce, brown sugar, and water. Pulse until well combined. Transfer to a medium-size saucepan and add the lime zest.

Bring the coconut milk mixture to a boil over medium heat. Add the tempeh cubes and stir gently to coat. Lower the heat to medium-low, cover the saucepan, and simmer for 20 minutes. Remove from the heat and let the tempeh cubes cool in the liquid mixture.

Remove the tempeh cubes from the liquid and thread them onto skewers.

Strain the liquid and reserve it.

Make the dipping sauce: In a medium-size saucepan, combine all the sauce ingredients with the reserved coconut milk mixture. Bring to a boil over medium heat and cook until thickened, about 4 minutes.

Brush the satay skewers with the sesame oil. Grill, turning often, for 4 to 6 minutes, or until browned on all sides. Serve promptly with ramekins of the dipping sauce on the side.

YIELD: 8 servings

SATAY SKEWERS

1 medium shallot, quartered

1 stalk lemongrass, sliced into 1-inch pieces (optional)

1 (1-inch) piece fresh ginger, peeled and sliced into coins

1 clove garlic, peeled

1 cup reduced-fat coconut milk

2 teaspoons chili sauce, such as sriracha, or the hot sauce of your choice

2 teaspoons brown sugar

½ cup water

3 slices lime zest

2 (8-ounce) packages tempeh, cut into 1-inch cubes

3 tablespoons toasted sesame oil

DIPPING SAUCE

¼ cup peach jam

2 tablespoons freshly squeezed lime juice

1 teaspoon soy sauce, or to taste

¼ cup water

Fiery Baby Artichokes

As if you didn't already know, playing with fire can be fun! (Just don't tell the kiddies that.) These little marinated rascals take so well to the grill you may never boil or steam them again. Grilling really concentrates that wonderful and elusive artichoke flavor. And by starting these baby artichokes in a microwave oven, you'll save at least a half hour in prep time.

Heat the grill to medium.

Cut the artichokes in half lengthwise and rub them with the lemon juice. In a microwave-safe casserole dish, combine the artichokes with any remaining lemon juice and the remaining ingredients. Cover tightly with plastic wrap. Microwave on high for 5 minutes. The timing for microwaving the artichokes will vary according to the wattage of your microwave, but start testing for doneness after 5 minutes.

Remove the dish from the microwave and turn the artichokes. Cover again with plastic wrap and cook for 2 minutes longer. They should be almost totally cooked before heading to the grill.

Remove the dish from the microwave again and carefully pull off the plastic wrap. Take the artichokes out to the grill and grill them for 3 to 5 minutes, turning once. Test for doneness with a toothpick. Serve warm.

If desired, serve the artichokes with ramekins of vegan mayonnaise (store-bought, or see pages 77 and 156) or another dipping sauce of choice.

YIELD: 2 servings

4 baby artichokes (about 2 ounces each), round bottom leaves removed, tough leaf tips trimmed

Juice of 1 lemon

½ cup vegan vegetable broth

¼ cup extra-virgin olive oil

Garlic powder

Onion powder

¼ teaspoon coriander seeds

¼ teaspoon crushed cardamom pods

1 teaspoon yellow mustard seeds (or black mustard seeds if you want it hotter)

Kosher salt

2 tablespoons extra-virgin olive oil

2 teaspoons garlic powder

2 teaspoons onion powder

1 pound fresh large white mushrooms

1 red bell pepper, stemmed, halved, and seeded

4 (8-inch) whole wheat pita rounds

½ to 1 cup Minty Pesto (see recipe and note)

Mushrooms & Peppers over Minty Pesto Triangles

Mushrooms are one of the easiest (and most forgiving) vegetables to grill. Their earthy flavor conveniently blends with pretty much any other ingredients, making them a favorite go-to grilling companion. Brushing these large white mushrooms with olive oil is always a must before they go on the grill, but when combined with garlic powder and onion powder, the sizzling mushrooms and red bell peppers assume a golden brown hue and are a perfectly seasoned match for the homemade Minty Pesto.

Heat the grill to medium-low.

In a small bowl, whisk together the olive oil, garlic powder, and onion powder. Brush the mushrooms and pepper halves with the mixture. Grill the vegetables until they're golden brown, 8 to 10 minutes, turning once. Transfer to a cutting board and thinly slice the mushrooms and the pepper halves. Toss them together and keep warm.

Place the pita rounds on the grill and toast lightly, about 3 minutes on each side. Watch carefully, as pita can burn quickly. Cut each pita round into eight triangles. You should then have thirty-two pieces.

Spread a few teaspoons of the Minty Pesto on each triangle and top with a portion of the warm mushroom mixture. If they've cooled off, run them briefly under a hot broiler or over indirect heat on the grill.

YIELD: 32 mushroom-pita triangles

minty pesto

In a food processor, combine all the ingredients. Pulse and process until you reach the consistency you prefer.

YIELD: About ½ cup

¾ cup fresh basil leaves

⅓ cup fresh mint leaves

2 tablespoons toasted sliced almonds (see toasting directions on page 85)

2 tablespoons extra-virgin olive oil

2 teaspoons freshly grated lemon zest

1 tablespoon freshly squeezed lemon juice

1 clove garlic, peeled and chopped roughly

Pinch of salt

Note: Depending on how much of the pesto you prefer to use, I suggest making a double batch, to equal 1 cup. Any leftover pesto will keep, tightly covered and refrigerated, for 3 to 4 days. It can also be frozen for 2 to 3 months, but will then lose a bit of its summery flavor.

3 tablespoons unpopped popcorn kernels

2 tablespoons canola oil

¼ cup extra-virgin olive oil, or to taste

½ teaspoon sea salt or kosher salt, or to taste

1 teaspoon smoked (Spanish) paprika

½ teaspoon garlic powder

½ teaspoon onion powder

½ teaspoon cayenne pepper, or more to taste

½ teaspoon dried oregano

½ teaspoon dried thyme

Drive-in Popcorn with Spanish Seasoning

For all those nights at the drive-in or when hosting a summer blockbuster in your own backyard, this unique homemade popcorn, for which you make your own nifty setup for grilling, utilizes a zippy bunch of spices that take the fluffy kernels in irresistible new directions.

Place the popcorn kernels and canola oil in a sturdy foil pie pan. Place another foil pan face down on top and wrap with heavy-duty aluminum foil to seal the pans together. Place the sealed pan on a hot grill, and use tongs to shake the pan occasionally, until you hear the corn begin to pop, then shake constantly to prevent burning the popped corn. The popcorn will be done in 8 to 10 minutes, by which time the popping sound will stop.

Immediately remove the pan from the grill and let rest for 1 minute, then carefully transfer the popcorn to a medium to large paper bag. Drizzle with the olive oil, and sprinkle with the sea salt, paprika, garlic powder, onion powder, cayenne, oregano, and thyme, then close and shake the bag vigorously. Serve at once in a bowl or other fun container.

YIELD: 2 to 4 servings

Chapter 4

SUMMERTIME
SALADS

Time to familiarize yourself with the following term: grilled salads. Yes, indeed, you will never look at tossed greens the same. Whether for a power lunch under the umbrella table where appearances are everything, or when towels and flip-flops are the dress code for the day, the next time it's much too hot for a feast with all the trimmings or you're entertaining a noontime gang of family and friends, grill up one or two of these light and easy dishes that are revolutionizing the traditional garden salad.

For as long as there have been grills, potato salad with mayo and egg has been the standard BBQ companion, but now a new generation of grilled greens is transforming how we create and enjoy picnic salads.

The list of salad ingredients here is expanded beyond just lettuce, tomato, and onion to fit everyone's taste for capturing summer in a bowl: leafy greens such as romaine, radicchio, and arugula are combined with the likes of fresh corn on the cob, eggplant, sweet potatoes, summer squash, portobellos, onions, and watermelon. Even the classic pasta salad gets a fiery makeover when fusilli and gemelli are introduced to grilled cherry tomatoes, zucchini, red peppers, and green onions.

Furthermore, grilled salads are the perfect chance to experiment and mix and match by layering exciting and unexpected new levels of flavors. Just imagine what happens when you toss spicy and bitter radicchio with balsamic portobellos or sweet potatoes are paired with green onions!

1 head romaine lettuce, well washed

2 tablespoons extra-virgin olive oil

1 tablespoon balsamic vinegar

2 teaspoons sunflower seeds, lightly toasted (see toasting directions)

2 teaspoons pine nuts, lightly toasted (see toasting directions)

Salt and freshly ground black pepper

To toast the sunflower seeds and pine nuts: In a dry cast-iron skillet over medium heat, place one layer of sunflower seeds. Lightly toast the seeds, shaking the skillet every 30 seconds, until they begin to brown. Repeat with the remaining sunflower seeds, then the pine nuts. Be especially careful with the pine nuts, as they burn easily. This can be done either over a stovetop or a gas or electric grill.

Romaine Holiday

This salad is a ridiculously simple and refreshing opener for any meal, whether you're entertaining a royal gone rogue or family and friends in the backyard. The gently wilted romaine sprinkled with balsamic vinegar is topped with toasted sunflower seeds and pine nuts, which especially contribute a nice textural contrast to get your meal off to a memorable start.

Heat the grill to medium-high.

Carve the romaine lettuce in half lengthwise. Leave the stem on, to hold the leaves together. Rub the lettuce halves all over with the olive oil.

Grill the lettuce halves for about 3 minutes per side, or until grill marks begin to appear. Divide between two serving plates; sprinkle with the balsamic vinegar, then with the toasted sunflower seeds and pine nuts. Salt and pepper the lettuce to taste, and serve.

YIELD: 2 servings

3 tablespoons extra-virgin olive oil, plus additional for rubbing the grill grates

1 red bell pepper, stemmed, seeded, and quartered

1 green bell pepper, stemmed, seeded, and quartered

1 yellow bell pepper, stemmed, seeded, and quartered

1 medium-size red onion, cut into ½-inch rings

2 yellow summer squash, stemmed and sliced in half lengthwise

2 zucchini, stemmed and sliced in half lengthwise

6 basil leaves, chopped finely

1 (14-ounce) can kidney beans, drained and rinsed

1 (8-ounce) jar artichoke hearts packed in oil, drained and rinsed

2 tablespoons red wine vinegar

Juice of 1 lime

1 tablespoon balsamic vinegar

Salt and freshly ground black pepper

August Salad

With its fiery shindig of bell peppers, red onion, summer squash, zucchini, artichoke hearts, and more, this gathering of garden veggies is the best of August in a bowl, which you can enjoy all year long.

Oil the grill grate and heat the grill to medium-high.

Grill the peppers, onion, squash, and zucchini in batches, using a grilling screen if necessary, until just lightly blackened and tender, turning once, about 8 minutes. Transfer the vegetables to a large bowl and let cool. When the vegetables are cool enough to handle, cut them with kitchen shears into bite-size pieces. Add the basil, kidney beans, and artichoke hearts to the bowl and toss to combine.

Whisk together the remaining 3 tablespoons of olive oil, red wine vinegar, lime juice, and balsamic vinegar. Pour the dressing over the vegetables and toss again. Season to taste with the salt and pepper and toss yet again.

YIELD: 6 to 8 servings

Portobello & Radicchio Salad

Few vegetables achieve deeper flavor from frolicking with a grill than portobellos. Yet when these mushrooms are bathed in a rich balsamic marinade for an hour or two before show time, their flavor is elevated to a whole new level, which then plays well with the bitter and spicy radicchio. As an added bonus, the simple prep here allows more time for you to kick back and bask in the sunlight.

In a medium-size bowl, whisk together the balsamic vinegar, onion powder, garlic powder, brown sugar, salt, and pepper.

Wash the portobellos and remove the black gills, if you wish. Pat the mushrooms dry with paper towels. Place the mushrooms gill side up in a baking dish or rimmed platter large enough to hold them in a single layer. Ladle the marinade into each mushroom cap and pour any remaining marinade into the dish, around the mushrooms. Cover the dish and refrigerate for 1 to 2 hours.

Oil the grate if necessary, then heat the grill to medium. Brush the tops of the mushrooms with the olive oil and place them on the grill, gill side up. Grill for 4 to 5 minutes, then turn the mushrooms carefully (they may splatter). Grill for 4 minutes longer. Remove the mushrooms from the grill and place them on a work surface. When just cool enough to handle, cut the mushrooms into bite-size pieces with kitchen shears.

Whisk together the remaining ¼ cup of olive oil with the red wine vinegar. In a large bowl, toss the radicchio leaves with the olive oil mixture. Add the mushrooms and toss again. Serve at once.

YIELD: 4 servings

½ cup balsamic vinegar

¼ teaspoon onion powder

¼ teaspoon garlic powder

2 pinches of brown sugar

Pinch of salt

Pinch of freshly ground black pepper

4 large portobello mushrooms, stems removed

¼ cup extra-virgin olive oil, plus additional for brushing the mushrooms

2 tablespoons red wine vinegar

1 medium-size head radicchio lettuce, stemmed, leaves washed and dried and torn into bite-size pieces

String Bean
& Arugula Salad

In this unusual pairing, the string beans and baby arugula work wonders for each other. Wilting the arugula with the hot, garlicky grilled beans is a nice trick for bringing the two together. While you can use regular arugula if you must, baby arugula is far milder in flavor, so try to find it if you can.

Heat the grill to medium-high.

In a large bowl, toss the string beans with the olive oil and garlic. Let the beans rest for 10 minutes or so, then place the beans on a large square of heavy-duty aluminum foil. Fold the foil over the beans and fold down the ends of the foil twice. Place the foil packet on the grill, seam side up, and grill for 25 to 30 minutes. Let the beans cool for a few minutes, then combine them in a roomy bowl with the arugula, lemon zest, and salt and pepper to taste, tossing until the arugula is wilted, 2 to 3 minutes.

YIELD: 3 to 4 servings

¾ pound green and/or yellow string beans, trimmed

3 tablespoons extra-virgin olive oil

2 cloves garlic, peeled and pressed

2 cups baby or regular arugula, trimmed and chopped

1 teaspoon finely grated lemon zest

Salt and freshly ground black pepper

SALAD

2 red bell peppers, stemmed and seeded, cut into long ½-inch-wide strips

2 white eggplants, stemmed and quartered lengthwise

2 leeks, stemmed, washed thoroughly, and quartered lengthwise

16 medium-thick asparagus stalks, trimmed

1 yellow summer squash, carved into chunks

1 zucchini, carved into chunks

12 baby red and/or white potatoes, washed and quartered

1 to 2 cups purchased flavored vegan croutons (optional) or homemade croutons (recipe follows)

DRESSING

½ cup extra-virgin olive oil

¼ cup dry white vermouth or dry white wine

1 teaspoon fresh thyme leaves

1 teaspoon minced fresh tarragon leaves

1 teaspoon chopped fresh sage leaves

1 tablespoon minced fresh cilantro leaves, or parsley, if you prefer

Salt and freshly ground black pepper

Farmers' Market Medley

Served at a backyard power lunch, a neighborhood pot-luck, or as part of a family night feast on the deck, this marinated garden of grilled red bell peppers, baby pota-toes, eggplants, leeks, asparagus, summer squash, and zucchini will always taste like it's fresh from the local farmers' market, even when it's not.

Heat the grill to medium-high.

Prepare the vegetables: In a large bowl, combine the pepper strips, eggplants, leeks, asparagus, squash, and zucchini. Place the potatoes in a separate bowl.

Prepare the dressing: In a blender, combine all the dressing ingredients. Pulse until smooth. Pour the dressing over the mixed vegetables and over the potatoes, tossing both well.

Place the potatoes on the grill rack. Cook, turning often, for about 10 minutes, or until the potatoes are tender. Transfer the potatoes to a large bowl. Grill the remaining vegetables for about 10 minutes, or until tender, using a large grill basket or grilling screen if necessary. Transfer the vegetables to the bowl with the potatoes and toss well. Just before serving, add the optional croutons and salt and pepper to taste, and toss again.

YIELD: 4 servings

To make homemade croutons: Trim and cube a loaf of hearty vegan white bread; toss the cubes in a large sauté pan over medium-high heat with ample drizzlings of good olive oil and, at the very end, chopped fresh herb(s) of choice, until toasty; or bake the oiled cubes on a sheet for 10 minutes or so at 375°F, stirring and turning halfway through. As another alternative, also see the grilled homemade croutons used for the Onion Rings with Garlicky Croutons on page 72.

Tattooed Watermelon Salad

Believe it or not, watermelon takes to grilling surprisingly well. The grill-inked stripes from the grate look beautiful and wild adorning the deep pink flesh, and they also nicely complement the seasoned arugula. Oftentimes guests, as I do myself, prefer two slices of the watermelon, to make the juicy joy of this fun in the sun rebel last as long as possible, so plan accordingly. Also, for a change, a sprinkling of smoked sea salt adds a whole other dimension to the dish.

Heat the grill to medium-high.

Cut the watermelon into eight 1-inch thick slices. Leave the rind on or cut it off, as you wish. Brush the watermelon flesh with 2 tablespoons of the olive oil. Season lightly with salt and pepper. Grill the watermelon for 2 minutes on each side. Mind the heat; liquid tends to gush out of the watermelon if it gets too hot. When finished, transfer the slices to four to eight plates.

Place the arugula in a medium-size bowl. Toss with the remaining 2 tablespoons of olive oil, then with the balsamic. Divide the arugula either under or over the watermelon slices. Sprinkle the watermelon with the smoked sea salt, if desired, and serve.

YIELD: 4 to 8 servings

1 medium-size seedless watermelon (about 5 pounds)

4 tablespoons extra-virgin olive oil

Salt and freshly ground black pepper

2 ample cups arugula leaves, or watercress leaves

2 tablespoons balsamic vinegar

Smoked sea salt of choice, for sprinkling (optional; see headnote)

SALAD

2 large sweet potatoes, peeled

4 green onions, left whole

Extra-virgin olive oil, for brushing
the vegetables

DRESSING

½ cup extra-virgin olive oil

1 tablespoon smooth vegan Dijon
mustard

¼ cup cider vinegar

2 tablespoons balsamic vinegar

2 teaspoons soy sauce

1 teaspoon pure maple syrup

1 teaspoon prepared horseradish

2 tablespoons chopped cilantro leaves,
or parsley

Salt and freshly ground black pepper

Sweet Potato & Green Onion Country Salad

A root vegetable often associated with holiday feasts, the sweet potato is a fairly new addition to the grill pantry. But just a little time spent over flames further accentuates the natural sweetness of this distant cousin of the potato. When guests ask where this beautiful and simple salad came from, just say it's a little something you whipped up at the last minute. And then explain how the green onions offset the sweetness of the potatoes, and how the dressing—*Oh, the Dijon–cider vinegar–soy sauce–maple syrup–and horseradish dressing!*—brings a welcomed conversation point to the dish.

Heat the grill to high.

Prepare the vegetables: In a medium-size saucepan in water to cover, boil the sweet potatoes for 20 minutes. Let cool, then cut into ½-inch slices. Brush the potato slices and green onions with the olive oil and place on the grill.

Grill the potatoes for 7 to 8 minutes, or until tender, turning once. Transfer the potatoes to a medium-size bowl.

Grill the green onions until softened, about 7 minutes, turning once. Remove the green onions, slice them thinly, and place them in the potato bowl.

Prepare the dressing: In a separate medium-size bowl, whisk together all the dressing ingredients. Pour the dressing over the potatoes and green onions, stirring to combine, and serve.

YIELD: 4 servings

Corn & Poblano Salad

For those carefree barbecues when plans go out the window and time is measured in laughs, this sunny caboodle of corn, poblanos, cherry tomatoes, onion, arugula, and tangy dressing leaves nothing to chance. Corn on the cob is one of the most exciting vegetables to grill when it comes into season. There's nothing like watching the tender, sweet kernels swell as the juice inside heats up and the vibrant yellow becomes emblazoned with crispy charred stripes. Although the corn here is husked before grilling, there are also benefits to leaving the husks on, which you'll see in the Grilled Corn on the Cob with Piquant Sauce on page 156.

Heat the grill to medium.

Prepare the vegetables: Rub the corn with the canola oil and season well with the salt and pepper. Grill the corn, turning every 2 minutes, for 8 minutes, or until the corn is getting browned. Remove the corn and set aside to cool.

When the corn is cool enough to handle, carefully remove the kernels into a large bowl with a sharp paring knife. After the kernels are removed, also scrape in the "milk" that remains behind the kernels from each ear.

Add the cherry tomatoes, poblano peppers, onion, and arugula to the corn bowl.

Prepare the dressing: In a medium-size bowl, whisk together all the dressing ingredients until well mixed. Pour the dressing over the corn mixture and toss well. Serve as soon as possible.

YIELD: 4 to 6 servings

SALAD

6 ears corn, husked

Canola oil, for rubbing the corn

Salt and freshly ground black pepper

2 cups cherry tomatoes, halved

2 poblano peppers, chopped into ½-inch pieces

1 medium-size red onion, chopped finely

2 cups baby arugula, or radicchio or romaine lettuce if desired

DRESSING

¼ cup extra-virgin olive oil

Juice of 1 lime

Salt and freshly ground black pepper

2 teaspoons paprika

1 teaspoon brown sugar

2 teaspoons onion powder

1 teaspoon garlic powder

1 teaspoon dried thyme

½ pound dried fusilli or gemelli

¼ cup extra-virgin olive oil

3 tablespoons red wine vinegar

1 teaspoon garlic powder

1 teaspoon onion powder

Salt and freshly ground black pepper

1 cup cherry or pear tomatoes

2 medium-size zucchini, quartered lengthwise

2 red bell peppers, seeded and cut into 2-inch strips

8 green onions, root ends trimmed, white and light green parts only

1 cup black olives, preferably kalamata, pitted

1 tablespoon chopped fresh oregano, or 2 teaspoons dried

2 tablespoons minced fresh basil leaves

Pasta Salad with Grilled Summer Vegetables

Screwy pasta gets dunked and splashed with color and gusto when paired with grilled cherry tomatoes, zucchini, red peppers, and green onions. Just remember, this pasta salad is best at room temperature, as chilling it tends to diminish the flavors.

Heat the grill to medium-high.

In a medium-size saucepan, cook the pasta in boiling water until just past al dente, according to the manufacturer's instructions, about 8 minutes. Drain and rinse to stop cooking. Transfer to a large bowl and toss with 1 tablespoon of the olive oil, to prevent the pasta from sticking together.

In a medium-size bowl, whisk the remaining olive oil with the red wine vinegar, garlic powder, onion powder, and salt and pepper to taste.

In a large bowl, combine the tomatoes, zucchini, bell peppers, and green onions. Pour the olive oil mixture over them and toss to coat well. You can also separate out the vegetables for coating, as they will be grilled separately momentarily. And, if desired, you can skip grilling the tomatoes and simply add them to the salad.

Transfer the zucchini and bell peppers to the hot grill rack. Grill for 3 minutes, turning once. Add the green onions to the grill rack and, using a grill basket if necessary, grill the tomatoes alongside the other vegetables for 3 to 4 minutes. Remove all the vegetables from the grill and let cool slightly.

Chop all the grilled vegetables into bite-size pieces and add them to the pasta bowl with the olives, oregano, basil, and any remaining marinade. Toss thoroughly and serve at room temperature.

YIELD: 6 to 8 servings

Chapter 5

FIRED-UP SIDES

Every great picnic feast needs a few captivating sidekicks. For your next flamed fete, stroll through this farmers' market of side dishes to find the perfect match for your grill—and your main course. Or, fire up several of these accomplices for a gratifying garden of choices that will indulge every guest's appetite.

Each of the following side dishes offers a savory balance to any meal; each is a classic vegetable side that has been reimagined with bursts of color, flavor, and flame—mushrooms smoked over a cedar plank, green beans dunked in a spicy Cajun sauce, grilled cauliflower sprinkled with paprika, plump juicy tomatoes charred to perfection, asparagus topped with a rich mandarin orange and pimiento sauce, and so much more.

With these dishes, it's never been easier to give your guests exactly what they want, especially as Mother Nature has already done most of the work here for you.

6 ounces cremini mushrooms, halved lengthwise

4 ounces oyster mushrooms, trimmed and cut into 1½-inch pieces

2 ounces chanterelle mushrooms, cut into 2-inch pieces

2 ounces shiitake mushrooms, stemmed and halved

1½ teaspoons Mushroom Crust (recipe follows)

¼ cup extra-virgin olive oil

1 tablespoon good balsamic vinegar

1 large shallot

1 teaspoon fresh thyme leaves

1 tablespoon fresh parsley (or cilantro, for a bit of a kick!)

Salt and freshly ground black pepper

Note: To prepare a new cedar plank for grilling, first season it by placing it on a preheated grill for 2 minutes, turning after 1 minute. Soak the plank for an hour in a bucket filled with water and 1 cup of dry white wine (or whatever wine you'll be serving with the meal) or apple juice. Place the marinated mushrooms directly on the plank, and grill with the lid closed, to smoke the mushrooms. There is no need to turn the mushrooms. Have on hand a spray bottle filled with water, in case the plank starts to burn.

Cedar-Smoked Mushrooms

The all-star lineup of cremini, oyster, chanterelle, and shiitake mushrooms gets the royal treatment when you combine it with a homemade mushroom crust, shallots, and herbs, and then grill using an easily prepared cedar plank. By all means, feel free to vary the quantities of the mushrooms. Chanterelles, after all, are a little pricey, so you can leave them out if need be.

Heat the grill to medium-high.

In a medium-size bowl, combine all the mushrooms with the Mushroom Crust. In a mini-processor, pulse the olive oil with the balsamic vinegar, shallot, herbs, and salt and pepper to taste. Pour this over the mushrooms and toss to coat well.

Arrange the mushrooms on a prepared cedar plank. Transfer to the grill, close the lid, and grill until the edges of the mushrooms are golden brown, about 12 minutes. Check the mushrooms and the plank every few minutes, but do it quickly to keep as much smoke under the grill lid as possible.

YIELD: 4 to 6 servings

mushroom crust

In a food processor, combine the dried mushrooms and pulse until coarsely ground. Add the remaining ingredients. Pulse until fine. Transfer to a small airtight container. Keeps up to 1 month.

YIELD: About ½ cup

3 tablespoons ground dried porcini mushrooms

3 tablespoons ground dried morel mushrooms

2 teaspoons coarse salt

¼ teaspoon freshly ground white pepper

1½ teaspoons dried thyme

1 tablespoon finely chopped lemon zest

ASPARAGUS

Canola oil, for brushing the asparagus and the grill.

1 pound fresh asparagus, trimmed

¼ cup toasted pine nuts (optional) (see toasting directions on page 52)

MANDARIN ORANGE & PIMIENTO SAUCE

1 (11- to 12-ounce) can mandarin oranges in juice, drained and chopped roughly

½ cup chopped pimiento

2 green onions, white and light green parts only, trimmed and chopped

1 tablespoon soy sauce

1 tablespoon toasted sesame oil

1 teaspoon finely chopped fresh ginger

Midsummer Night's Asparagus with Mandarin Orange & Pimiento Sauce

This whimsical asparagus dish boasting a playful mandarin orange and pimiento sauce is certainly an unusual amalgamation of flavors and textures. Perfect for those steamy late-night suppers, this side dish or light tapas will leave you and your fellow nature sprites wondering if the fantastic feast you just had was real or a mere figment of your appetite.

Brush the grill grate with the canola oil, then heat the grill to medium.

In a small bowl, combine all the sauce ingredients. Set aside.

Brush the asparagus with the canola oil. Grill the asparagus just until tender crisp, 4 to 5 minutes. Drain. Divide the asparagus among 2 or 3 plates. Spoon the mandarin and pimiento mixture over the asparagus and sprinkle with the optional pine nuts.

YIELD: 2 to 3 servings

4 large yellow onions, unpeeled

⅔ cup extra-virgin olive oil

Kosher salt

2 slices vegan Tuscan bread,
¾ inch thick

1 clove garlic, unpeeled and halved

¼ cup fresh parsley leaves

3 tablespoons freshly squeezed
lemon juice

Onion Rings with Garlicky Croutons

As the song goes, "Love is a burning thing" (indeed!), and now to the delight of smoldering appetites everywhere so is mealtime, especially when accompanied by these grilled onion rings on the side. With a sprinkling of parsley and homemade garlicky croutons, this dish possesses a deepness of flavor that you don't usually get with yellow onions.

Heat the grill to medium.

Slice off the ends of each onion so that you can see the rings. Cut the onions crosswise into ¾-inch to 1-inch slices, keeping the rings intact and the skins on as much as possible. Brush all cut sides of the onions with 4 tablespoons of the olive oil and sprinkle with the kosher salt. Grill the slices until tender and caramelized, 10 to 15 minutes per side (20 minutes in all if you're using an indoor grill). If the onions burn, just scrape off the charred portion (a little charring tastes good). Let the onions cool.

Meanwhile, make the croutons: Grill the bread until toasted on both sides, then rub all over with the cut sides of the garlic and sprinkle with 2 tablespoons of the olive oil and kosher salt. Cut the bread into crouton-size pieces.

When the onions have cooled, remove the remaining skins and separate the onions into rings. Divide among four plates and sprinkle with the parsley and the croutons. Drizzle with the lemon juice and the remaining olive oil. Serve hot or at room temperature.

YIELD: 4 servings

Grilled Sesame Snow Peas

This is about the only form of *snow* that's welcome when firing up the barbie, though grilling in the heart of winter certainly is sweet revenge on Jack Frost as he's nipping at your nose. For these snow peas, toasted sesame oil is the dominant flavor when it comes to melting your hunger away. However, this oil is strong, so you may want to use less than what's suggested.

In a dry cast-iron skillet over medium heat (on either a stovetop or gas or electric grill), toast the sesame seeds, shaking the pan often, until the seeds begin to brown. Immediately transfer the seeds to a bowl and let cool.

Heat the grill to medium.

In a small bowl, whisk the rice wine vinegar with the sesame oil, soy sauce, brown sugar, garlic powder, and ginger.

Place the snow peas on a large sheet of heavy-duty aluminum foil. Pour the vinegar mixture over the peas. Fold and seal the packet. Grill the packet for 8 to 10 minutes, or until tender (check after 8 minutes).

Transfer to a serving bowl, sprinkle with the toasted sesame seeds, and serve promptly.

YIELD: 4 servings

---

1 tablespoon sesame seeds

¼ cup rice wine vinegar

2 teaspoons toasted sesame oil

2 teaspoons soy sauce

1 tablespoon brown sugar

½ teaspoon garlic powder

1 teaspoon grated, peeled fresh ginger

1 pound snow peas, fresh or frozen (thaw if frozen)

Grill-Kissed Cauliflower with Smoked Paprika

Cauliflower benefits particularly from a little R & R on the grill because it brings out all sorts of hidden sweetness in this often-underappreciated vegetable. And when seasoned with smoked paprika, the result is quite simply beautiful and mouthwatering.

Heat the grill to medium or medium-high.

Remove the stem and leaves from the cauliflower. Wash the head well and pat it dry with paper towels. Rub the olive oil all over the cauliflower and sprinkle it with the seasoned salt and the paprika. Let the cauliflower rest for a few minutes, then wrap it fairly tightly in heavy-duty aluminum foil.

Grill the cauliflower for about 45 minutes, or until it's as tender as you like it, testing with a long toothpick.

Unwrap the head, carve it, and break it into florets. Serve warm.

Or, break the cauliflower into florets, season, and place the seasoned cauliflower florets directly on the grill grate for several minutes, turning occasionally until golden and browned.

YIELD: 4 servings

1 medium-size head cauliflower

¼ to ½ cup extra-virgin olive oil

2 teaspoons seasoned salt, such as Lawry's

2 teaspoons smoked paprika (see note)

Note: Smoked paprika is usually Spanish, but non-Spanish editions have been cropping up around America. If you can't find smoked paprika, just use regular paprika, but it won't be quite as good.

BEANS

1 pound whole green beans

1 tablespoon canola oil

Salt and freshly ground black pepper

CAJUN SAUCE

6 tablespoons vegan mayonnaise
(store-bought, or see recipe
that follows)

1 tablespoon smooth vegan Dijon
mustard

1 teaspoon Cajun Seasoning
(see recipe that follows)

1 teaspoon kosher salt

½ teaspoon freshly ground
black pepper

*Note: Make the Cajun sauce a day ahead
of time to let the flavors blend.*

Crispy Green Beans
with Cajun Sauce

The humble green bean practically jumps right out of the garden and onto the grill just to revel in the fiery, homemade Cajun sauce of this simple and Big Easy side dish.

Heat the grill to medium-high.

Prepare the beans: In a large bowl, toss the green beans with the canola oil and season with the salt and pepper to taste. Place the beans in a large grilling basket and set the basket on the grill rack.

Grill until the beans are charred on the bottom, then flip the basket to cook the other side of the beans, about 4 minutes per side.

Meanwhile, make the Cajun sauce. In a small bowl, combine all the sauce ingredients, mixing well. Depending on your preference for sauce, I suggest doubling this recipe in case your guests prefer extra. Any leftover sauce will keep, tightly covered and refrigerated, for 3 to 4 days.

Transfer the beans to a platter and serve with ramekins of the Cajun sauce.

YIELD: 5 to 6 servings

cajun seasoning

In a medium-size bowl, combine all the ingredients and stir well.

YIELD: About ¾ cup

homemade vegan mayonnaise

In a medium-size saucepan, stir together the flour, sugar, water, and vinegar. Cook over medium-low heat, stirring often, until thick.

In a standing blender, combine the vegetable oil, lime juice, zest, salt, dry mustard, and tofu, and blend well.

Add half of the hot flour mixture to the blender and blend. Add the remaining flour mixture and blend again.

Use at room temperature or cooled in the refrigerator. Homemade mayonnaise will keep in the refrigerator for 4 to 5 days.

YIELD: About 2 cups

CAJUN SEASONING

3 tablespoons paprika

2 tablespoons kosher salt

1 tablespoon freshly ground black pepper

1 tablespoon freshly ground white pepper

1 tablespoon onion powder

1 tablespoon garlic powder

2 teaspoons dried thyme

1 teaspoon cayenne, or more to taste

HOMEMADE VEGAN MAYONNAISE

¾ cup all-purpose flour

½ cup sugar

1 cup water

½ cup cider vinegar

¾ cup vegetable oil

2 tablespoons freshly squeezed lime juice

1 teaspoon grated lime zest

2 teaspoons salt

½ teaspoon dry mustard

¾ cup soft tofu, pressed and drained, if desired (see page 14)

4 ripe but fairly firm tomatoes, halved crosswise

Kosher salt

Freshly ground black pepper

Extra-virgin olive oil

8 fresh basil leaves, cut into chiffonade (see note)

Note: To cut basil leaves into a chiffonade, place the leaves in a single stack and roll them up like a cigar. Hold them in place and slice them thinly with a sharp paring knife.

Grilled Tomato Suns

This side dish is the ideal way to add a pop of color and interest to any meal. When tomatoes rise into their peak season, around August, lunge for this recipe! Just be sure the cherry red orbs aren't too soft, though, or they'll collapse from overheating (dramatic little divas, aren't they?).

Over your kitchen wastebasket or compost bin, use your little finger to wiggle out the tomato seeds and pulp from the pockets inside the tomatoes.

Heat the grill to high heat.

Season the tomatoes well with the kosher salt and pepper, and rub the cut sides with the olive oil. Using a fine grill grate (if possible) or grilling screen, place the tomatoes, cut side down, over high heat. Cover the grill and let the tomatoes cook for about 4 minutes, checking for doneness after 2 minutes. (The rate of cooking will depend on the ripeness of the tomatoes, among a few other factors.) Lift the tomatoes off the grill with a thin metal spatula.

Place the tomatoes on a serving platter, cut side up. Drizzle with a little more olive oil and sprinkle on a bit more salt and pepper. Finish with a showering of basil chiffonade.

YIELD: 4 to 8 servings

4 Yukon Gold potatoes, sliced into
1-inch chunks

¼ cup extra-virgin olive oil

2 tablespoons garlic powder

Salt and freshly ground black
or white pepper

Chunky Grilled Potatoes

Your guests will be panning the buffet table for these
shiny nuggets at your next party. Grilling the Yukon
Golds with a generous dusting of garlic powder will not
only get the dinner rush started, it will reconfirm that
garlic powder does indeed have its uses.

Bring the grill to high heat.

In a medium-size bowl, toss the potato slices with the olive oil.
Toss them again with a tablespoon of the garlic powder, then
toss them yet again with the remaining garlic powder and salt
and pepper to taste. Cover the bowl tightly and set it aside for
3 hours.

Grill the potatoes for 5 minutes, then turn and grill for 5 minutes more, or until the potatoes are fairly tender.

YIELD: 4 servings

Spicy Corn with Black Beans & Zucchini

Fresh corn and zucchini add charred flavor to spicy black beans that have been amped up with jalapeño, garlic powder, paprika, and a splash of dry white wine. The secret here is grilling the corn with the inner husks left on, which creates a nice grassy flavor that heralds summer with every bite. And, if you really want a mouthy bonfire, by all means add another jalapeño.

Remove the outer husks, but leave the tender inner husks on to cover the corn kernels. Soak the corn in water stirred with the sugar for ½ hour.

Meanwhile, heat the grill to medium.

On a stove, place 2 tablespoons of the olive oil in a roomy sauté pan over medium heat and cook until the oil slides easily across the bottom of the pan, about 1 minute. Add the onion and jalapeño. Cook for 2 to 3 minutes, or until the vegetables just start to soften. Add the garlic powder, onion powder, paprika, ketchup, and salt and pepper to taste. Cook, stirring, for 2 minutes longer. Add the beans and a splash of the wine, lower the heat, and simmer the mixture for 15 to 20 minutes, adding more wine if the bean mixture dries out.

While the beans cook, grill the corn until the husks are browned. Then remove from the grill and let cool slightly.

Slice the zucchini into thirds lengthwise and brush with the remaining olive oil. Grill the zucchini slices for 2 to 3 minutes per side, until grill marks develop.

Cut the kernels off the corncob and add to the bean mixture. Slice the zucchini into bite-size pieces and stir into the bean mixture. Serve warm.

YIELD: 4 servings

1 ear unhusked corn

¼ cup sugar

¼ cup extra-virgin olive oil

½ medium-size white onion, diced

1 jalapeño, stemmed and minced

1 teaspoon garlic powder

1 teaspoon onion powder

1 teaspoon paprika

1 tablespoon ketchup

Salt and freshly ground black pepper

1 (14-ounce) can black beans, drained

¼ cup dry white wine

2 medium-size zucchini (about ½ pound)

Crackling Kale, Swiss Chard & Red Bell Pepper

When cabbagelike kale, leafy Swiss chard, and red bell peppers come together for this A-list side dish, you'll not only be keeping up with the Joneses, you'll be stealing the show altogether. Kale and Swiss chard are especially durable enough to grill without losing their wonderful leafiness. Also, note that darker green chard has a stronger flavor than the lighter leafed variety, so choose according to your preference.

Wash the kale and chard and chop into bite-size pieces. In a large bowl, toss them well with a generous amount of the olive oil, then toss with (to taste): kosher salt, pepper, garlic powder, and powdered ginger.

Spread the greens mixture on a large sheet of heavy-duty aluminum foil. Form an airtight pouch with the foil. However, the pouch itself should be loose, so the greens inside can steam.

Heat the grill to medium. Place the foil pouch on the grill grates, place the bell pepper nearby, and close the grill lid. Grill for 10 to 12 minutes, turning the bell pepper with tongs every 2 to 3 minutes.

Remove the bell pepper and the aluminum pouch. Carefully open the pouch and sprinkle the warm greens with the lemon juice.

When it's just cool enough to handle, stem and seed the pepper and slice it into attractive strips.

Toss the greens with the pepper strips and serve.

YIELD: 1 large portion or 2 to 3 side dishes

1 large bunch kale

1 bunch Swiss chard stalks

Extra-virgin olive oil

Kosher salt

Freshly ground black pepper

½ teaspoon garlic powder, or to taste

½ teaspoon powdered ginger, or to taste

1 red bell pepper

Juice of 1 lemon

Note: This is a "per-person" recipe. Figure on about three good handfuls of kale and chard per person.

6 sprigs fresh rosemary, leaves pulled from stems and chopped

⅓ cup extra-virgin olive oil

Salt and freshly ground black pepper

2 pounds red potatoes, well washed and quartered

Potatoes with Rosemary

The point here is quite simple: No herb dresses up potatoes with more verve than piney fresh rosemary. This is a super-easy side dish that will quickly become a frequent attraction at your dinners and picnics.

Heat the grill to medium.

In a large bowl, place the chopped rosemary leaves, olive oil, and salt and pepper to taste. Whisk well to combine.

Add the quartered potatoes and stir to coat all the potatoes with the olive oil mixture.

Place the potatoes on the grill rack and grill for about 20 minutes, turning occasionally, or until tender.

YIELD: 6 servings

Simple Broccoli with Toasted Almonds

Even self-proclaimed broccoli haters fall head over flip-flops for this side dish. Grilling gives the tepidly flavored broccoli a real power boost, and the toasted almonds add a touch of nutty elegance.

Prepare the grill for indirect heat using a drip pan (see page 9). Oil the grill racks if necessary.

Place the broccoli in a large bowl. In a smaller bowl, whisk together the olive oil with the lemon juice and salt and pepper to taste. Pour the mixture over the broccoli and toss to coat. Let the broccoli stand for 30 minutes.

Toss the broccoli again, then drain off the marinade. Place the broccoli on the grill grates over the drip pan and grill, covered, for 18 to 20 minutes, turning once, until the broccoli is crisp-tender.

Slice the broccoli into bite-size pieces and transfer to a large bowl. Pour in the almonds and toss to combine. Serve at once.

Or, as a charred alternative, coat bite-size florets with extra-virgin olive oil, season with salt and pepper to taste, and place them on a grill grate or grilling screen over direct medium heat, turning as needed, for several minutes, until tender on the inside and blackened and crispy on the outside.

YIELD: 6 servings

---

6 cups fresh broccoli floret clusters, well rinsed

2 tablespoons extra-virgin olive oil

3 tablespoons freshly squeezed lemon juice

Salt and freshly ground black pepper

1 cup toasted almonds (see toasting directions)

To toast almonds: Place 1 cup of almonds in a skillet large enough to hold them in about one layer, over medium-high heat, and shake the skillet every 30 seconds, until the almonds are lightly browned, or browned to your liking. This can be done either over a stovetop or a gas or electric grill.

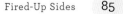

Chapter 6

TAPAS ON THE DECK

Whether you're throwing a barefoot cocktail party or inviting a few friends over for a splash in the pool or a long overdue powwow around the campfire, these tapas, or light snacks, are portioned so they can be served with no fuss on individual little plates, perfect for an umbrella table or laps.

Dishes such as grilled eggplant in a homemade hoisin sauce, artichokes with a cumin dipping sauce, balsamic-glazed zucchini, grilled corn on the cob slathered in a lime and pepper sauce, portobellos with roasted leeks and spinach, and a loaded baked potato are meant to be light enough to suffice for a casual bite between friends, yet still filling enough to either tide everyone over until mealtime or serve as a light meal themselves.

Featuring unique flavor combos and playful textures, one or two of these garden-fresh dishes will do for a few friends, but a lineup of several grilled tapas down the picnic table or scattered around the beach blanket will let everyone know that you have the monopoly on sun 'n' fun (but that you're willing to share)!

As a bonus, these dishes pair well with everything from beer and wine to whatever else your guests might fancy from the Happy Hour taking place around the clock in Chapter 12.

Flame-Glazed Eggplant with Hoisin Sauce

Your guests will be glazed over with satisfaction when they bite into these slices of marinated pleasure. The homemade hoisin sauce gives this hearty eggplant many strata of flavor—the soy sauce, peanut butter, molasses, white vinegar, orange zest, and seasonings convene in one spirited mixture, while the toasted sesame oil in particular adds a nice smoky background—but be careful, it's strong stuff!

Heat the grill to medium.

In a medium-size bowl, whisk together the hoisin sauce, garlic, soy sauce, rice wine, sesame oil, and 1 tablespoon of the canola oil.

Brush the eggplant slices on both sides with the remaining tablespoon of canola oil and season judiciously with kosher salt. Grill until browned and tender, about 5 minutes, turning once.

Brush the eggplant slices on both sides with the hoisin marinade, and grill for 1 minute on each side, to thicken the glaze. Serve at once.

YIELD: 4 servings

homemade hoisin sauce

In a small bowl, combine all the ingredients, mixing well.

YIELD: ¼ cup

¼ cup hoisin sauce (store-bought, or see recipe that follows)

2 cloves garlic, peeled and pressed

2 tablespoons soy sauce

1 tablespoon rice wine

2 teaspoons toasted sesame oil

2 tablespoons canola oil

1 large eggplant, cut lengthwise into 1-inch thick slices, scored lightly on both sides in a crisscross diamond pattern

Kosher salt

HOMEMADE HOISIN SAUCE

4 tablespoons soy sauce

1 tablespoon vegan peanut butter, or to taste

1 tablespoon molasses or brown sugar

2 teaspoons white vinegar

⅛ teaspoon garlic powder

⅛ teaspoon onion powder

1 teaspoon orange zest (for great background flavor)

2 teaspoons toasted sesame oil

Hot sauce of choice

⅛ teaspoon freshly ground black pepper, or to taste

Note: When shopping for hoisin sauce or peanut butter, be sure to check the ingredient list to make sure the brand you're buying is vegan.

4 large artichokes
(3 to 3½ pounds total)

2 lemons

2 tablespoons extra-virgin olive oil

¼ teaspoon salt

Freshly ground pepper

Vegan mayonnaise, for serving
(store-bought, or see pages 77
and 156)

Ground cumin, for flavoring the
vegan mayonnaise (optional)

*Note: Grilled artichokes will keep, tightly
wrapped in foil or plastic, refrigerated for
1 day. They're pretty good chilled, but most
people prefer them warm.*

Artichokes with Cumin Dipping Sauce

Hailing from the Mediterranean, artichokes are most often served steamed, but grilling them adds a welcomed snap of smokiness to their flavor profile. If you can get them, early-season baby artichokes will yield extra-tender results, but then double the number of artichokes per person and reduce the cooking time.

Choose a saucepan large enough to hold all the artichokes. Place the artichokes in the pan and cover them with cold water. Squeeze in the juice of one of the lemons. One at a time, trim the leaves from the top of an artichoke and remove the tough outer layer of leaves. Trim the bottom of the stem and, using a vegetable peeler, peel off the outer layer of the whole stem. Return the artichoke promptly to the lemon water and proceed with the remaining artichokes.

When all the artichokes are ready, cover the pan and bring the water to a boil. Boil until the base of the stem can be pierced with a fork, about 15 minutes, depending on the size of the artichokes. Transfer the artichokes to a cutting board and let them cool for about 10 minutes.

Heat the grill to medium.

Slice the artichokes in half lengthwise. With a grapefruit spoon (or regular spoon), scoop out the choke of each artichoke and the first few inner layers in the center, until the bottom is revealed. Brush each half lightly with the olive oil and sprinkle with salt and pepper to taste. Grill the artichokes until they're tender and lightly charred, about 5 minutes per side. Transfer them to a serving platter, and squeeze the remaining lemon over them. Serve warm or at room temperature, with ramekins of the mayonnaise stirred with the optional cumin (to taste) for each person.

YIELD: 4 servings

CORN

2 tablespoons canola oil

¾ teaspoon chili powder (see note)

¼ teaspoon salt

4 ears corn, husked

LIME & PEPPER SAUCE

⅓ cup vegan mayonnaise
(store-bought, or see pages 77
and 156)

3 tablespoons chopped fresh cilantro
or parsley leaves

1 teaspoon garlic powder

¼ teaspoon ground pepper

¼ teaspoon cayenne pepper

4 teaspoons freshly squeezed
lime juice

*Note: If you can't find a good chili powder,
just add another ¼ teaspoon of cayenne.*

Grilled Corn on the Cob with Lime & Pepper Sauce

By now, thanks to the corn recipes on pages 63 and 81, the marvels of grilling these sweet, golden cobs have been well established. Here, a spirited homemade vegan mayonnaise, infused with cilantro, garlic powder, ground pepper, cayenne, and freshly squeezed lime juice, steals the show. Be sure to slather the corn with the sauce as soon as the corn is removed from the grill, and then lose yourself as you work your way down row after row of plump, glistening kernels.

Heat the grill to medium.

Prepare the corn: In a small bowl, stir together the canola oil, chili powder, and salt, and rub the mixture all over the corn. Grill the corn, turning every 2 minutes, for 8 minutes, or until the corn is browning.

Meanwhile, make the sauce. In a medium-size bowl, mix the mayonnaise with the remaining sauce ingredients. Coat the corn with the mixture as soon as it's off the grill and cool enough to handle.

YIELD: 4 servings

Balsamic-Splashed Zucchini

Summer would not be the same without the highly anticipated debut of zucchini at roadside vegetable stands and farmers' markets. And there's no need to waste time once the summer squash appears. This ultra-easy dish reconfirms that nothing perks up zucchini better than a hot grill and a good splashing of balsamic vinegar.

Heat the grill to medium-high.

Slice the zucchini in half lengthwise, then cut the lengths in half crosswise. Brush the cut sides with 2 tablespoons of the olive oil and sprinkle with the salt and pepper.

Place the zucchini, cut side down, on an oiled grill and cook for 5 minutes. Turn over the zucchini and grill for 3 to 5 minutes or until tender. Transfer the zucchini to a platter and arrange in a single layer. Lightly splash with the balsamic vinegar. Sprinkle the basil and chervil on top. Drizzle with the remaining olive oil and finish with a sprinkling of salt and pepper.

YIELD: 4 servings

4 small zucchini

2 tablespoons extra-virgin olive oil, plus 1 to 2 tablespoons, for drizzling

½ teaspoon coarse salt

½ teaspoon freshly ground pepper

1 tablespoon balsamic vinegar

1 tablespoon chopped fresh basil

1 tablespoon chopped fresh chervil or tarragon

Vegetables on a Picnic

Grilling invokes a natural sweetness in these vegetables, and combines it toothsomely with that unbeatable smokiness. With this pile of sunny day veggies, ants won't be the only ones clamoring to hop on your picnic blanket; friends and strangers alike will all be angling for a nibble.

In a medium-size bowl, combine the olive oil with the garlic, thyme, sage, and rosemary. In a roomy baking pan, place the eggplants, zucchini, squash, onion, and bell pepper, and brush with the olive oil mixture. Let marinate for at least 2 hours, or preferably overnight.

Heat the grill to medium-high. Season the vegetables with the salt and pepper to taste. Grill just until tender, about 8 minutes, turning once. Serve warm.

YIELD: 4 to 6 servings

¼ cup extra-virgin olive oil

3 cloves garlic, peeled and pressed

2 teaspoons chopped fresh thyme leaves

2 teaspoons chopped fresh sage leaves

2 teaspoons chopped fresh rosemary leaves

2 medium-size Japanese eggplants, halved lengthwise

2 medium-size zucchini, halved lengthwise

2 medium-size yellow squash, halved lengthwise

1 medium-size red onion, cut into ½-inch slices

1 red bell pepper, stemmed, seeded, and quartered

Salt and freshly ground black pepper

1 pound medium to large asparagus spears, trimmed and soaked in cool, lightly sugared water for a few hours

½ pound portobello mushrooms, stems discarded, black gills scraped out, cut in half

1 red or yellow bell pepper, halved and seeded

¼ cup extra-virgin olive oil

2 teaspoons fresh rosemary leaves, chopped

1 teaspoon kosher salt

½ teaspoon freshly ground black pepper

2 teaspoons good balsamic vinegar

2 teaspoons white truffle oil (optional)

Tossed Asparagus, Portobellos & Peppers

Grilling asparagus is one of the very best ways to coax the maximum flavor from these stately spears. Coupling it with hearty portobello mushrooms and a bell pepper for this tapas is, indeed, an unexpected hookup, once more proving that variety on the grilled veggie circuit is the spice of life. Also, soaking asparagus in lightly sugared water—about 1 tablespoon per quart—restores some of the sweetness they lose in the hours after they're harvested.

Heat the grill to medium-high.

In a large bowl, toss the asparagus, mushrooms, and peppers with the olive oil, rosemary, kosher salt, and pepper until the vegetables are coated with the oil. Spread the vegetables on the hot grates and grill for 10 to 15 minutes, turning often.

Once removed from the grill, chop the portobellos, bell pepper, and asparagus into bite-size pieces and toss with the balsamic vinegar and truffle oil.

YIELD: 4 servings

Grill-Baked Potatoes

These easy flame-baked potatoes, grilled to perfection over a grate or open campfire, are a meal in and of themselves, especially when served loaded with a colorful selection of vegan Cheddar cheese or nutritional yeast, green onions, chives, salsa, and anything else you might want to pile on.

Heat the grill to medium-high.

Prepare the potatoes. There are two ways of grilling the potatoes. On a grill only, wrap the potatoes in aluminum foil and position them about 4 inches above the heat source for 1 hour to 90 minutes, or until desired doneness, turning every 15 to 20 minutes. Or, on a microwave-safe plate, microwave the potatoes on high for 8 minutes (turn them after 4 minutes), or until they are tender. Place the potatoes on the grill. Cook for 10 to 15 minutes to desired doneness, turning occasionally.

For campfire-baked potatoes: Wrap the potatoes in aluminum foil. Place the wrapped potatoes in the red-hot coals of the campfire. If you prefer the potato shell to be blackened, place the potatoes in the hot coals without aluminum foil. Bake the potatoes for 20 to 30 minutes, or until desired doneness, watching carefully. Be careful to not burn yourself when removing and opening the packets.

Split the cooked potatoes and serve with the Cheddar cheese or nutritional yeast, green onions, chives, seasoned salt, salsa, and any other toppings of choice.

YIELD: 4 servings

4 baking potatoes, scrubbed, pierced, rubbed with extra-virgin olive oil, and sprinkled with salt

TOPPINGS

½ cup shredded vegan Cheddar cheese or nutritional yeast

¼ cup chopped green onions

¼ cup chopped fresh chives

Seasoned salt, such as Lawry's

Vegan salsa (store-bought, or see Salsa Grand Slam on page 148)

- 1 large red bell pepper
- 1 large yellow bell pepper
- 2 poblano peppers
- 4 tablespoons extra-virgin olive oil
- Kosher salt and freshly ground black pepper
- 8 ounces soft and crumbly vegan cheese of choice
- 1 medium-size head Bibb lettuce
- 1 tablespoon balsamic vinegar

Cheesy Grilled Peppers on Bibb Lettuce

This simple and elegant tapas takes advantage of the embellishment of flavor that occurs when whole bell peppers are left on a grill to blacken. Not only does the flame add its own smokiness to the bells, it also emboldens their innate sweetness, which is evident when the charred skin is later rubbed away. When the peppers are then sliced and laid atop fresh Bibb lettuce that's been sprinkled with balsamic vinegar and olive oil and grill-softened vegan cheese, the resulting snack can also double as a light salad course.

Heat the grill to high. Grill all four peppers, turning often, until blackened on all sides. Transfer the peppers to a roomy bowl and cover tightly with plastic wrap. Let the peppers steam for 15 minutes, then rub off most of the blackened skin with paper towels. (Don't rinse the peppers after rubbing off the blackened skin, or they'll lose a lot of flavor.)

Place the peppers on a cutting board. Stem all the peppers, then open each one and pull out all the seeds. Slice the peppers into ½-inch strips. Drizzle with 2 tablespoons of the olive oil and season well with the salt and pepper.

Crumble the cheese and place it on a small raft of aluminum foil. Place the foil on the grill, cover the grill, and heat until the cheese begins to soften, 1 to 2 minutes.

Place several lettuce leaves on four plates, drizzle with the remaining 2 tablespoons of olive oil, and sprinkle with the balsamic vinegar. Divide the softened cheese among the plates. Scatter the peppers over all and serve at once.

YIELD: 4 servings

Canola oil, for oiling the grill rack

2 small onions, each cut into 8 wedges

24 whole okra pods (about ¾ pound), trimmed

16 cherry tomatoes (about ½ pound)

4 teaspoons extra-virgin olive oil

½ teaspoon dried thyme

½ teaspoon dried rosemary, crumbled with your fingers

½ teaspoon dried oregano

1 teaspoon kosher salt

1 teaspoon freshly ground black pepper

1 teaspoon water

½ teaspoon ground red pepper

⅛ teaspoon sugar

2 cloves garlic, minced

Okra, Tomato & Onion Kebabs

It's time to do a little social climbing to the grilled life. To help you are some bona fide veggie elite: okra, cherry tomatoes, and onion wedges brushed with an olive oil and herb medley. As for the okra, people who say they don't like this vegetable probably feel that way because the okra they've had was slimy—a texture it can easily achieve if it's not properly cooked. Here on the grill, okra keeps its fairly firm texture and a soothing flavor. Bamboo skewers are especially showy with this trio, but just remember to soak the wooden skewers in water first for at least 20 to 30 minutes.

Oil the grate with the canola oil, and then heat the grill to medium-high.

Divide each onion wedge into two equal pieces. Thread alternately three okra pods, two cherry tomatoes, and two onion pieces onto each of eight 12-inch skewers.

In a small bowl, combine the olive oil, thyme, rosemary, oregano, salt, pepper, water, red pepper, sugar, and garlic, and whisk the mixture well.

Brush the olive oil mixture over the skewered okra, tomatoes, and onions. Place the skewers on the rack. Grill for 3 minutes on each side or until tender.

YIELD: 8 skewers, 4 to 8 servings

Portobellos with Roasted Leeks & Spinach

This snack is a refreshing new twist on an old friendship, pairing the portobellos' earthy flavor with a classic balsamic vinaigrette, but this time with the addition of roasted leeks and spinach. Known as ramps in the wild, leeks are a favorite way to add an edge to any dish when you want to give onions and garlic a rest. When used as part of the stuffing for these mushroom caps, the balsamic-coated leeks fill the tapas with their distinct flavor and balance the overall flavor profile of the dish by infusing the mushroom itself.

Chop off the root ends of the leeks (use white and light green parts only). Slice them crosswise into ½-inch coins and transfer to a bowl of cold water. Swish the leeks with your hands to release the dirt. Lift the leeks out of the water and pour away the water with the grit. Repeat this process until you no longer see any grit. Drain the leeks in paper towels.

In a large bowl, combine the olive oil, balsamic vinegar, and salt and pepper to taste, and whisk well. Add the leeks and spinach leaves to the oil mixture and toss to coat thoroughly.

Heat the grill to medium-high.

Rub the mushroom caps with the olive oil and grill them, gill side down, for 2 to 3 minutes. Turn over the caps, fill them with the leek mixture, and divide the cheese among the four caps. Close the grill and cook the stuffed mushroom caps for 7 to 8 minutes, until the cheese begins to brown. Serve warm.

YIELD: 4 servings

2 leeks

3 tablespoons extra-virgin olive oil, plus additional for rubbing the mushrooms

3 tablespoons balsamic vinegar

Kosher salt and freshly ground black pepper

2 cups chopped fresh spinach leaves

4 portobello mushroom caps

1 cup crumbly vegan cheese of choice, or nutritional yeast

Chapter 7

COUNTRY MARINADES FOR TOFU, TEMPEH & SEITAN

Tofu, tempeh, and seitan are the ultimate blank canvases when it comes to grilling. When painted with generous strokes of marinades and sauces, be they sweet or fiery, these happy campers are just as delish climbing up a skewer with veggies for a snack or light meal as they are performing alone on a grill for a hearty main course.

For parties, consider preparing several of the marinades that follow, such as the classic Finger-Lickin' BBQ Sauce, Asian Infusion, Lemon & Garlic Sittin' on a Skewer, Brown Sugar & Bourbon, Baby!, Bonfire of the Herbs, Mustard ♥ White Wine, Pineapple Does the Teriyaki, Mamma Mia!, Drop It like It's Hot Sauce, and Merry Margarita. Then, either invite your guests to engage their inner culinary artist at a DIY kebab bar stocked with a variety of bite-size tofu, tempeh, and/or seitan, and vegetables, or surprise them grillside with a smorgasbord of your own creations.

Also, kebabs are an especially fun way to introduce children and veggie-curious guests to this tasty threesome.

Unless otherwise noted, each of the marinades and sauces that follow work well with at least 8 ounces of unflavored tofu, tempeh, or seitan. Naturally, the marinade amounts can always be doubled or tripled for larger parties. Some of the marinades with larger yields already work well for parties and when prepping larger amounts of this dynamic trio. Just remember the following:

Press and drain firm/extra firm tofu before grilling (see page 14); tempeh benefits from a pregrill simmer in water or vegan vegetable broth (see page 16); and seitan, because of its sometimes crumbly nature, works best on a grilling screen when sans skewer.

Place the tofu, tempeh, or seitan and the marinade in either a resealable plastic bag or nonreactive container, such as glass. Marinate all three for several hours to overnight—the longer the better. Then, while grilling, continue to brush on the leftover marinade or sauce as desired. Because marinades tend to be ooey, gooey, and runny, you may want to grill on aluminum foil, a grilling screen, or use a grill pan for easy cleanup.

All grills are different, so the cooking times for tofu, tempeh, and seitan may differ slightly from the following directions, depending on your grill and heat level. Therefore, the best rule of thumb is to always watch the food closely while grilling, turn it every few minutes, and follow your instincts.

Grilling times over medium to high heat are roughly as follows:

Tofu kebabs: 8 to 10 minutes, or until the tofu is golden and crispy, and the vegetables are tender. Turn every minute or two.

Tofu slices (cut as desired) alone: 8 to 10 minutes, or until golden and crispy. Turn once or twice.

Tempeh kebabs: 8 to 10 minutes, or until browned, and the vegetables are tender. Turn every minute or two.

Tempeh slices (cut as desired) alone: 8 to 10 minutes, or until browned. Turn once or twice.

Seitan kebabs: 8 to 10 minutes, or until browned and crispy, and the vegetables are tender. Turn every minute or two.

Seitan slices (cut as desired) alone: 8 to 10 minutes, or until browned and crispy. Turn once or twice.

For kebabs, let your imagination run wild. In addition to the tofu, tempeh, and seitan, add any combination of onions, mushrooms, zucchini, bell peppers, asparagus, or other vegetables and even fruit that are in season. If you're at a loss for which vegetables and fruits to include, peruse your local farmers' market, roadside vegetable and fruit stands, or refer to the "Grilling Times for Fruits and Vegetables" chart at http://grillingtips.com for inspiration. Just remember, the more colorful and daring, the more memorable! And, if using bamboo skewers, don't forget to soak them in water for at least 20 to 30 minutes ahead of time, to prevent burning.

When marinated tofu, tempeh, or seitan flies solo, pair it with a fitting side dish (see Chapter 5) for a main dinner course, or add it to a favorite garden salad or sandwich for lunch.

Finally, it can be fun to create your own marinades. So feel free to experiment with the following recipes by adding a pinch of a favorite seasoning or a nearby herb. Remember, you're the artist here. Now go, and create those masterpieces.

For all the marinades, except the Finger-Lickin' BBQ Sauce, follow these basic directions: In a medium-size bowl, combine all the marinade ingredients, mixing well. Combine the tofu, tempeh, or seitan (cut as desired) and the marinade in a resealable plastic bag or nonreactive container, mixing well, and refrigerate the mixture, covered, for several hours to overnight, turning the tofu, tempeh, or seitan occasionally. Then grill according to the approximate times and methods described. All the marinades will keep in a covered container in the refrigerator for 3 to 4 days.

Four Oranges

Sweet, spicy, and herbal all at the same time! *And* with a swig of Cointreau, to boot. With this marinade, you and your guests will always be in a sunshine state of mind.

YIELD: About ½ cup

Asian Infusion

For this spicy Asian marinade, soy sauce, rice wine, horseradish, and the rest of the gang will really raise the roof at your next barbecue.

YIELD: About ½ cup

FOUR ORANGES

2 tablespoons extra-virgin olive oil

1 tablespoon freshly squeezed orange juice

1 teaspoon orange oil

1 tablespoon orange marmalade

2 tablespoons Cointreau

1 tablespoon chopped fresh cilantro

1 teaspoon red pepper flakes, or to taste

ASIAN INFUSION

2 tablespoons soy sauce

2 tablespoons rice wine vinegar

1 tablespoon rice wine

1 teaspoon minced, peeled fresh ginger

1 teaspoon toasted sesame oil

1 teaspoon garlic powder

1 teaspoon onion powder

1 teaspoon prepared horseradish

1 teaspoon Chinese five-spice powder

**LEMON & GARLIC
SITTIN' ON A SKEWER**

1 tablespoon canola oil

2 teaspoons soy sauce

2 tablespoons freshly squeezed
lemon juice

1 tablespoon finely minced lemon zest

1 teaspoon garlic powder

1 teaspoon dried thyme

Freshly ground white pepper
(to taste)

KING WASABI

1 teaspoon prepared wasabi mustard

2 tablespoons maple syrup

2 tablespoons canola oil

2 teaspoons soy sauce

1 teaspoon powdered ginger

1 tablespoon cognac

Lemon & Garlic
Sittin' on a Skewer

A classic love fest of flavors if ever there was one, lemon and garlic never disappoint.

YIELD: About ⅓ cup

King Wasabi

Almighty and powerful wasabi mustard leaves no question as to who rules the roost, when paired with maple syrup, ginger, and cognac for this high-octane marinade.

YIELD: About ⅓ cup

Bonfire of the Herbs

With a rich vanity "fare" of celery seed, basil, thyme, sage, bay leaf, and other seasonings, this spry marinade will bring out your inner herbivore every time it hits flame.

YIELD: About 1½ cups

Mustard ♥ White Wine

Dijon mustard and dry white wine blend beautifully with a posse of molasses, garlic, and soy sauce, proving that a love of good food is always in the air, and ready to sizzle.

YIELD: About 3 cups

BONFIRE OF THE HERBS

1 cup vegan vegetable broth

1 tablespoon pickling spice

½ teaspoon celery seeds

½ teaspoon dried basil

½ teaspoon dried marjoram

½ teaspoon dried thyme

½ teaspoon dried sage

1 bay leaf

3 peppercorns, crushed

¼ teaspoon allspice

2 tablespoons freshly squeezed lemon juice

¼ cup vinegar

MUSTARD ♥ WHITE WINE

1 cup vegan Dijon mustard

1 cup dry white wine

¾ cup extra-virgin olive oil

¼ cup molasses

1 clove garlic, minced

2 tablespoons soy sauce

1 cup ketchup

2 shallots, minced

1 clove garlic, peeled and pressed

¼ cup vegan Worcestershire sauce
(store-bought, or see recipe
that follows)

Juice of 1 lemon

2 teaspoons molasses

2 teaspoons malt vinegar

1 teaspoon kosher salt

1 teaspoon prepared mustard,
vegan Dijon preferred

1 teaspoon crushed red pepper

½ teaspoon Tabasco sauce

2 pinches of dried thyme

**HOMEMADE VEGAN
WORCESTERSHIRE SAUCE**

2 cups cider vinegar

½ cup soy sauce

¼ cup light brown sugar

1 teaspoon powdered ginger

1 teaspoon dry mustard

1 teaspoon onion powder

1 teaspoon garlic powder

½ teaspoon ground cinnamon

½ teaspoon freshly ground
black pepper

Finger-Lickin' BBQ Sauce

No barbecue is complete without an appearance by this legend of the grilling circuit, which especially transforms tempeh and seitan into finger-lickin' rock stars.

In a small saucepan, combine all the ingredients and simmer over low heat for 10 minutes. Remove from the heat and let cool.

The sauce will keep for 10 days, refrigerated.

YIELD: 1½ cups

homemade vegan worcestershire sauce

In a medium-size saucepan, combine all the ingredients over medium-high heat. Bring to a boil, then lower the heat to simmer and reduce the mixture by half, about 20 minutes. Strain through a fine sieve and let cool completely before using. The sauce will keep in a tightly covered container, refrigerated, for 2 to 3 months.

YIELD: About 1 cup

Pineapple Does the Teriyaki

PINEAPPLE DOES THE TERIYAKI

1¼ cups pineapple juice

¼ cup vegan Worcestershire sauce (store-bought, or see page 108), or dry red wine or sherry

1 tablespoon liquid smoke

¼ cup soy sauce

1 tablespoon extra-virgin olive oil

1 teaspoon powdered ginger

½ teaspoon garlic powder

½ teaspoon onion powder

Pineapple juice supercharges traditional ingredients to let your guests know, beyond a doubt, why your glowing embers are the hottest on the block. For kebabs, consider adding a few pineapple chunks to the skewer for an additional rhythm of excitement, or serve the teriyaki kebabs with the Grilled Pineapple Rings on page 189.

YIELD: About 1¾ cups

Orange & Lime Summer Juice

ORANGE & LIME SUMMER JUICE

¼ cup freshly squeezed lime juice

¼ cup freshly squeezed orange juice

2 tablespoons cider vinegar

½ teaspoon dried thyme

1 clove garlic, minced

½ teaspoon seasoned salt, such as Lawry's

¼ teaspoon chili powder

Lime juice and OJ once more prove their status as summertime staples when paired with thyme, garlic, and chili powder for a marinade that will have your kebabs dancing right off the grill and into happy mouths.

YIELD: About ¾ cup

Apple Cider Harvest

Especially nice for autumn grill fests, this marinade hits a tangy crescendo, playing well to the crowd that likes a punch of seasonings on its food. Cue the falling leaves and harvest moon.

YIELD: About 1 cup

Prime-Time Lime

Lime adds a pucker punch of flavor to brown sugar, garlic, and red pepper flakes, for a marinade that will dominate the headlines at your next grill bash.

YIELD: About 1¼ cups

APPLE CIDER HARVEST

¾ cup apple cider vinegar

2 teaspoons vegan Worcestershire sauce (store-bought, or see page 108), or dry red wine or sherry

1 teaspoon ground cumin

1 teaspoon cayenne pepper

2 teaspoons dry mustard

1 teaspoon powdered ginger

1 clove garlic, minced

1 medium-size onion, chopped

PRIME-TIME LIME

⅓ cup freshly squeezed lime juice

½ cup vegan vegetable broth

1 teaspoon grated lime zest

2 tablespoons extra-virgin olive oil

1 tablespoon brown sugar

2 cloves garlic, minced

⅛ teaspoon crushed red pepper flakes

Brown Sugar & Bourbon, Baby!

This wickedly sophisticated bourbon blend can really perk up virtually anything. I especially love to marinate firm tofu in it before grilling. Remember, though, bourbon is flammable, so be ready with a water spritzer if need be.

YIELD: About ½ cup

2 tablespoons soy sauce

3 tablespoons bourbon

1 tablespoon brown sugar

1 teaspoon cayenne pepper

1 teaspoon onion powder

1 teaspoon garlic powder

Apple of My Eye

APPLE OF MY EYE

¼ cup apple juice concentrate

¼ cup white wine vinegar

2 tablespoons soy sauce

2 tablespoons olive oil

1 teaspoon crushed fresh savory

Refreshing and savory, this beloved apple juice marinade is especially tempting with seitan, but also cavorts well with tofu and tempeh.

YIELD: About 1 cup

Lemon & Pepper Boogie-Woogie

LEMON & PEPPER BOOGIE-WOOGIE

1 teaspoon lemon zest

½ cup freshly squeezed lemon juice

⅓ cup extra-virgin olive oil

2 tablespoons chopped green onions

4 teaspoons sugar

1½ teaspoons salt

1 teaspoon vegan Worcestershire sauce (store-bought, or see page 108), or dry red wine or sherry

1 teaspoon prepared mustard, vegan Dijon preferred

1 teaspoon freshly ground pepper

Two old buddies, lemon and pepper, come together here to show they've still got what it takes to electrify their fans, especially when in cahoots with onions, mustard, and vegan Worcestershire sauce, or dry red wine if you prefer.

YIELD: About 1 cup

Mamma Mia!

When paired with tempeh and seitan in particular, this simple and classic homemade Italian marinade will leave even your most discerning guests, and Mom, declaring "It's *amore!*"

YIELD: Nearly 2 cups

Get Tangy with It

Kick it up a notch by hitting the grill with a high note of soy sauce, dry mustard, pepper, parsley, and garlic powder for a real backyard blowout.

YIELD: Nearly 3½ cups

MAMMA MIA!

1 tablespoon dried oregano

1 tablespoon garlic powder

1 tablespoon salt

1 tablespoon freshly ground pepper

2 tablespoons freshly squeezed lemon juice

1½ cups extra-virgin olive oil

GET TANGY WITH IT

1½ cups vegetable oil

¾ cup soy sauce

½ cup vegan Worcestershire sauce (store-bought, or see page 108), or dry red wine or sherry

2 tablespoons dry mustard

⅓ cup vinegar

1 tablespoon freshly ground pepper

1¼ teaspoons salt

1 teaspoon dried parsley

⅓ cup freshly squeezed lemon juice

1 teaspoon garlic powder

¼ cup freshly squeezed lemon juice

¼ cup freshly squeezed lime juice

¼ cup extra-virgin olive oil

1 tablespoon grated orange zest

1 teaspoon dried rosemary

1 clove garlic, minced

½ teaspoon salt

½ teaspoon freshly ground pepper

Lemon, Lime & Orange

Lemon, lime, and orange are victorious every time these superfoods join their marinating powers to defeat the evil pangs of hunger.

YIELD: A little over ¾ cup

¼ cup dry sherry

¼ cup soy sauce

2 tablespoons sesame oil

1 tablespoon grated fresh ginger

1 clove garlic, minced

DROP IT LIKE IT'S HOT SAUCE

1 (0.7-ounce) packet Good Seasons Italian Dressing (powder)

½ cup (1 stick) vegan margarine

2 cups Frank's Red Hot Cayenne Pepper Sauce

4 to 6 tablespoons beer (optional)

Oh, Sherry!

Sherry, sesame oil, and ginger provide very powerful flavor profiles for this marinade that meshes nicely over a grill in what will be an edible love triangle you'll want to be right in the middle of.

YIELD: Nearly ¾ cup

Drop It like It's Hot Sauce

Especially powerful with tempeh and seitan—when you wrap your mouth around kebabs coated with this blazing sauce, you'll see fireworks! Yes, the ingredients may surprise you, but their quick and simple blending will become one of the easiest and hottest tricks up your sleeve at grill time. This homemade lava is also tasty over grilled, meatless chik'n products (see page 19) for a quick lazy day meal or snack.

YIELD: About 2½ cups

Drunken Kebabs

Starring red wine and beer, this marinade will satisfy every guest's preference for one or the other as they get to imbibe their way down the soused skewer.

YIELD: 4 cups

Merry Margarita

Something tells me these orange liqueur–and–tequila-infused kebabs will be gone in a flash!

YIELD: A little over ¾ cup

DRUNKEN KEBABS

2 cups red wine

12 ounces beer

1 small red onion, sliced

Juice from 6 to 8 limes

¼ cup chopped fresh cilantro

½ teaspoon salt

¼ teaspoon freshly ground pepper

¼ teaspoon red pepper flakes

¼ teaspoon ground cumin

MERRY MARGARITA

2 tablespoons orange liqueur

¼ cup tequila

2 cloves garlic, minced

½ teaspoon salt

2 tablespoons freshly squeezed lime juice

¼ cup extra-virgin olive oil

1 jalapeño, seeded and minced

¼ cup fresh cilantro, chopped

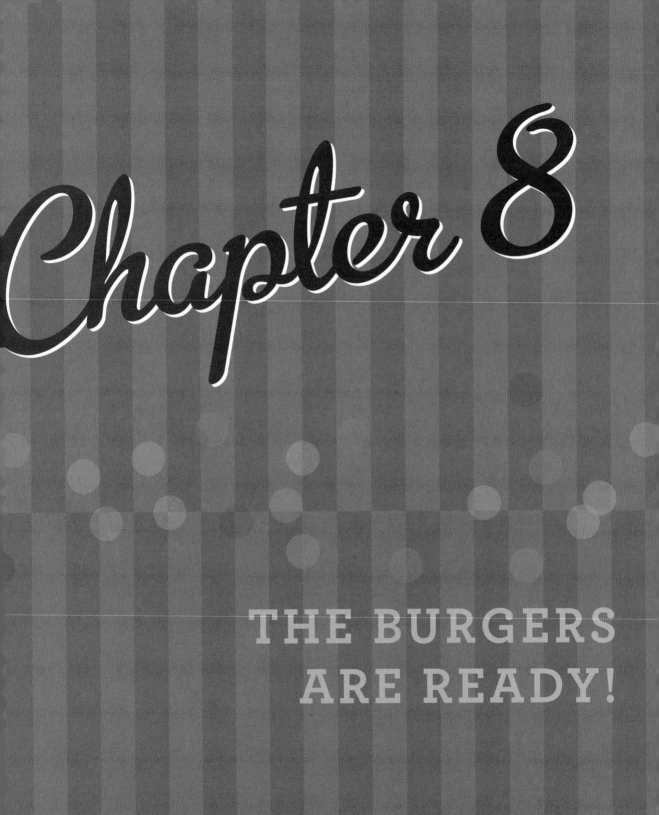

Chapter 8

THE BURGERS ARE READY!

"*The* burgers are ready!" Ahhhh, rarely are more beautiful words uttered in the great outdoors. Beefy burgers have long ruled the grill circuit, but not everyone got to join in the fun. Talk about poetic justice—now, thanks to this collection of innovative veggie burgers, some with international "flare" indeed, no bun will ever again be left empty on Flame Day.

My friends, *beefy* has just taken on a whole new meaning. And when it comes to flavor, just reading the ingredient lists that follow will be enough to send you racing for the grill. Packed with spices, herbs, and garden-fresh vegetables, the Slip-N-Siders, Mexican Tortilla Burgers, Southwestern Burgers with Salsa, Italian Herb Burgers on Focaccia, and other burgers here have an uncanny ability to turn any meal into a culinary journey.

You may be new to making your own veggie burgers, but it will become second nature once you start working with these fresh and vibrant ingredients. Granted, homemade veggie patties take a little extra time and effort, and you need to be careful not to overprocess the mixtures or else you'll end up with mush; but, trust me, you will reap many benefits with every bite.

If it's more of a noontime sandwich you're looking for, the second half of the chapter lays out just over a week's worth, taking advantage of such fresh gems as asparagus, avocados, pears, and broccoli. Not to mention an inspired new take on the BLT, and get ready to behold—grilled PB & J sandwiches!

1 (15-ounce) can garbanzo beans, drained and well rinsed

4 green onions, roots trimmed, white and light green parts only, chopped roughly

2 slices vegan sandwich bread, crusts trimmed, torn into pieces

⅓ cup toasted almonds (see toasting directions on page 85)

½ teaspoon ground cumin

½ teaspoon ground coriander

1 knob of ginger (about 1 tablespoon), peeled and roughly chopped

1 tablespoon soy sauce

2 tablespoons vegan egg substitute

3 tablespoons extra-virgin olive oil

8 vegan slider buns, preferably whole wheat

1 tablespoon smooth vegan Dijon mustard

⅓ cup vegan mayonnaise (store-bought, or see pages 77 and 156)

Slip-N-Sliders

Sliders are all the rage these days, especially for a light bite under the sun. This savory grilled version has layers of deep flavor—cumin, coriander, ginger, soy sauce—that you don't usually encounter in garbanzo preparations, guaranteeing you clear sailing every time.

Heat the grill to high.

In a food processor, combine the garbanzo beans, green onions, bread, almonds, cumin, coriander, ginger, and soy sauce. Pulse the mixture just until roughly chopped. Being careful of the processor blade, transfer half the mixture to a bowl. Add the egg substitute to the mixture in the processor and process until smooth, then transfer to the same bowl and mix thoroughly with the roughly chopped mixture.

Form the mixture into eight patties about ¾ inch thick, sizing them to fit into the slider buns. Brush all sides of the patties with the olive oil and, using a grilling screen if desired, grill until lightly blackened, about 8 minutes, turning once.

Serve the burgers in the slider buns with the mustard and mayonnaise.

YIELD: 8 sliders

Stacked Portobello Burgers

The mature *Agaricus bisporus* is one of the most generous vegetables when it comes to satisfying our cravings, especially for a hearty, stacked burger. Joined by a bevy of balsamic bell pepper wedges, tomatoes, onions, and romaine, the grilled portobellos anchor this burger when tucked into potato bread rolls.

In a large bowl, whisk the canola oil with the balsamic vinegar, garlic powder, onion powder, soy sauce, and half of the pepper. Add the bell pepper wedges and mushrooms, and toss to coat thoroughly. Marinate the mixture at room temperature for 30 minutes.

Lightly oil the grates, if necessary, then heat the grill to medium. Grill the pepper wedges, skin side down, until blackened, about 10 minutes. Set aside and let cool. Rub off the skins with paper towels.

Grill the mushrooms, covered, until tender, about 8 minutes, turning once.

Place two mushrooms on the bottom half of each hamburger roll and top with a bell pepper wedge, a lettuce leaf, and tomato and red onion slices. Close the burgers and serve promptly.

YIELD: 4 burgers

¼ cup canola oil, plus oil for the grill grate

¼ cup balsamic vinegar

2 teaspoons garlic powder

2 teaspoons onion powder

2 teaspoons soy sauce

1 teaspoon freshly ground black pepper

1 red bell pepper, stemmed and seeded, carved into 4 wedges

8 portobello mushrooms (about 1 pound), stemmed

4 vegan potato bread hamburger rolls, or regular vegan hamburger buns if desired

4 romaine lettuce leaves, trimmed to fit inside the rolls

1 ripe tomato, sliced

1 red onion, sliced

Mexican Tortilla Burgers

It's time to hang grillside with all your closest amigos. Just keep in mind, for these Mexican-inspired burgers to stay onboard in one pretty patty while surfing the grill, to finely mash the ingredients but resist the temptation to puree them (because that would be a total messy, mushy wipeout!). Also, the patties require some advance chilling time before grilling, which means you also get plenty of time to chill out, yourself!

In a food processor, place the beans, 1 cup of the oats, and the flour, egg substitute, shiitake caps, onion, pepper, carrot, garlic, soy sauce, kosher salt, cumin, paprika, chili powder, oregano, cilantro, lime juice, and hot sauce. Pulse until coarsely chopped, then add more oats, if needed, to help the burger patties hold together, pulsing the processor but not enough to puree the ingredients.

Chill the mixture for at least 1 hour, then shape them into 2-inch-diameter by ½-inch thick patties on a waxed paper–lined baking sheet. Chill the patties, covered loosely, for several hours, or overnight.

Heat the grill to medium-high.

Bring the patties to room temperature and broil them 5 inches from the heat source for 8 to 10 minutes, turning once, or until browned (watch them closely as less time may be required), checking to make sure the ingredients are holding together well. Broiling first will help prevent them from falling apart on the grill.

Reheat the patties on the grill, using a grilling screen if desired, while you lightly toast the corn tortillas, letting them remain pliable. Serve the burgers in the warmed tortillas with avocado slices, shredded lettuce, chopped tomato, chopped onion, and more of your favorite hot sauce.

YIELD: 4 servings

1 (14-ounce) can kidney beans, drained and rinsed well

1 cup old-fashioned rolled oats (use more or less, as needed)

½ cup all-purpose flour

¼ cup vegan egg substitute

6 shiitake mushroom caps, chopped finely

½ cup finely chopped onion

½ cup finely chopped red or green bell pepper

1 medium-size carrot, shredded

2 cloves garlic, peeled and pressed

1 tablespoon soy sauce

Kosher salt

1 teaspoon ground cumin

½ teaspoon smoked paprika

1 teaspoon chili powder

1 teaspoon dried oregano, or 2 teaspoons fresh

2 tablespoons chopped fresh cilantro leaves

A good squeeze of lime juice

A generous splash of your favorite hot sauce

8 to 10 vegan corn tortillas

2 ripe avocados, sliced

1 cup shredded lettuce

1 large tomato, chopped

1 medium-size onion, peeled and chopped

BURGERS

2 (19-ounce) cans garbanzos
(38 ounces in all)

2 teaspoons garlic powder

1 teaspoon onion powder

1 teaspoon tahini

2 tablespoons chopped fresh parsley

1 teaspoon ground cumin

1 teaspoon ground coriander

1 teaspoon kosher salt

1 teaspoon freshly ground
black pepper

1 pinch of curry powder,
or slightly more, to taste

½ cup whole wheat flour

Extra-virgin olive oil, for frying
before grilling

CREAMY LEMON TAHINI SAUCE

1 cup vegan sour cream (store-bought,
or see page 39)

2 teaspoons freshly squeezed
lemon juice

2 teaspoons tahini

1 teaspoon minced fresh dill

1 teaspoon minced mint leaves

1 medium-size cucumber, peeled,
seeded, and diced finely

Garbanzo & Herb Burgers with Creamy Lemon Tahini Sauce

The ever versatile garbanzos (chickpeas) here are blended with a rich assembly of favorite herbs and spices for zesty little disks sans buns. To top off these seasoned burgers in spectacular fashion is an unbelievably refreshing homemade Creamy Lemon Tahini Sauce that will be the envy of everyone who couldn't make it to the party.

Prepare the burgers: Drain the garbanzos and rinse them thoroughly. Pat dry with paper towels and transfer to a large bowl. With a potato masher, mash them roughly, leaving some of them whole for texture. Blend in the garlic powder, onion powder, tahini, parsley, cumin, coriander, kosher salt, pepper, and curry powder and mix well. Stir in the flour and mix well. Let the mixture rest for 20 minutes.

Meanwhile, make the tahini sauce: In a medium-size bowl, whisk the sour cream with the lemon juice. Whisk in the tahini, dill, and mint. Stir in the diced cucumber.

Form the rested chickpea mixture into 2-inch balls and flatten them into disks. You'll have 25 to 30 disks.

Heat the grill to medium-high.

On a stovetop, in a large skillet, fry the garbanzo patties in ½ inch of olive oil over medium-high heat for 3 minutes on each side. Transfer to a plate and take them to the grill. Using a grilling screen if desired, grill the patties for 1 to 2 minutes on each side. Be careful, as these burgers are delicate.

Serve with ramekins of the Creamy Lemon Tahini Sauce for spreading or dipping.

YIELD: About 6 to 8 servings

Southwestern Burgers with Salsa

Whether you're a real cowboy or cowgirl, or just pretending to be one for kicks, when it's time to get down-home on the grill, these burgers will add a Southwestern giddyap to any gathering with black beans, brown rice, toasted sunflower seeds, cumin, and chili powder. However, be careful not to overprocess the mixture, or your Wild West burgers may wimp out on you.

In a food processor, combine the beans, rice, garlic powder, sunflower seeds, red bell pepper, spinach, cilantro, kosher salt, cumin, and chili powder. Pulse just until the mixture becomes a chunky puree.

Heat the grill to medium-high.

In ¼-cup increments, form the mixture into patties about ¾ inch thick. Brush the patties all over with the canola oil and grill them, using a grilling screen if desired, for about 10 minutes on each side. Grill them well, but don't dry them out.

Meanwhile, lightly toast the sourdough buns on the grill.

Serve the burgers in the toasted sourdough buns, two patties per bun, with a good dollop of salsa in between the patties.

YIELD: 6 sandwiches

1 (15-ounce) can black beans, drained and rinsed

1 cup cooked and cooled brown rice

2 teaspoons garlic powder

½ cup lightly toasted sunflower seeds (see toasting directions on page 52)

1 medium-size red bell pepper, stemmed, seeded, and chopped

10 fresh spinach leaves, chopped roughly

2 tablespoons chopped fresh cilantro leaves

2 pinches of kosher salt, or to taste

1 teaspoon ground cumin

1 teaspoon chili powder, or to taste

Canola oil, for brushing the patties

6 vegan sourdough buns

Your favorite vegan bottled salsa, for serving (or see Salsa Grand Slam on page 148)

1 (15-ounce) can kidney beans

1 to 2 cups old-fashioned rolled oats, as needed

½ cup all-purpose flour

¼ cup vegan egg substitute

½ cup roughly chopped white mushrooms

½ cup roughly chopped red onion

1 carrot, shredded

½ cup roughly chopped red bell pepper

4 cloves garlic, peeled and pressed

4 fresh basil leaves, chopped roughly

1 teaspoon dried oregano

2 tablespoons chopped fresh parsley leaves

¼ cup well-chopped sun-dried tomatoes

2 tablespoons tomato paste

1 tablespoon soy sauce

Vegan focaccia bread, for serving

Note: If you can't find focaccia, grill up some vegan whole wheat pita bread instead and proceed.

Italian Herb Burgers on Focaccia

Life doesn't get much sweeter than a grill surrounded by good friends and laughter, and topped with these Italian-inspired focaccia burgers. Here, fresh mushrooms, red onion, bell pepper, garlic, basil, oregano, parsley, sun-dried tomatoes, and other ingredients belt out an opera of flavors we can all sink our teeth into.

In a food processor, combine all the ingredients, except the focaccia. Pulse until just coarsely chopped, adding more oatmeal as needed (start with 1 cup), until the mixture holds together when you make a patty.

Chill the mixture for an hour. Shape into patties about ½ inch thick and about 4 inches in diameter. Chill the patties on a plastic wrap–covered platter for at least 3 hours.

Heat a broiler and a grill to medium-high. Broil the patties about 5 inches from the heat source for 4 to 6 minutes, or until lightly browned (watch them closely, as times may vary), checking to make sure the ingredients are holding together well. Broiling first will help to prevent them from falling apart on the grill. Using a grilling screen if desired, transfer the patties to the heated grill and grill for 2 to 3 minutes, turning once.

Serve at once, with the focaccia bread.

YIELD: Varies, but enough for 3 to 4 people

½ cup instant couscous or quinoa

Pinch of kosher salt, plus extra

¼ cup freshly squeezed lemon juice

1 to 2 teaspoons minced lemon zest

1 tablespoon fresh thyme leaves

½ cup vegan mayonnaise
(store-bought, or see pages 77
and 156)

Freshly ground black pepper

16 asparagus spears, not too thin
or too thick, stems trimmed

½ sweet onion, such as Vidalia, peeled
and sliced ¼ inch thick

2 tablespoons extra-virgin olive oil

4 vegan whole wheat pita breads,
for serving

Asparagus, That's a Wrap!

Whether served on a beach blanket or picnic blanket, these asparagus spears wrapped snuggly with zesty couscous and onion are always ready for their tasty close-up.

Heat the grill until hot.

On the stovetop, in a medium-size saucepan, bring ¾ cup of water to a boil. Add the couscous with the pinch of the kosher salt. Stir once. Remove from the heat, cover, and let stand about 5 minutes. Fluff the couscous with a fork to prevent clumping.

In a medium-size bowl, combine the lemon juice and zest, thyme, and mayonnaise with the couscous. Season to taste with kosher salt and pepper.

Slice off the tough ends of the asparagus spears. In a large bowl, combine the asparagus with the sliced onion and olive oil. Season lightly with kosher salt and pepper.

Grill the asparagus and onions until the onions are soft and browned, about 10 minutes. Be sure the asparagus and onions are cooked until tender.

Divide the couscous over the tops of the pita bread. For each of the four wraps, place four asparagus spears over the couscous, and one-quarter of the grilled onion on top of the asparagus. Roll up each pita tightly and seal with a toothpick.

YIELD: 4 servings

Tomato Bread

Piled with garlic, onion, eggplant, zucchini, yellow squash, and red bell peppers and set atop baby arugula, grilled Tomato Bread is a close BFF to bruschetta that will especially impress the ladies and gents who lunch, or a pool full of hungry youngsters.

Heat the grill to medium-high.

Brush the garlic head and the onion slices with the olive oil and place them on the outer edge of the grill to let them cook slowly. Grill for about 8 minutes, turning the garlic every 2 minutes. Leave the garlic and onion on the grill while cooking the rest of the vegetables.

Cut the eggplant into thick slices. Brush the eggplant, zucchini, squash, and peppers lightly with the olive oil and place in the center of the hot grill. Cook for just 2 minutes on each side, until the vegetables are seared and starting to brown.

Cut the bread into ½- to ¾-inch slices and brush with the olive oil. Grill the bread on both sides just until brown. Cut the tomato in half and rub over one side of each bread slice. Discard the tomato.

Divide the baby arugula among four serving plates. When the garlic has grilled and softened, slice off the top of the head with a sharp knife. Squeeze the soft garlic into a small bowl, and spread on one side of each toasted bread slice. Divide the grilled vegetables and onion slices among the bread slices and serve on top of the baby arugula.

YIELD: 4 servings

1 large head garlic

1 large red onion, peeled and carved into ½-inch slices

Extra-virgin olive oil, for brushing

1 medium-size white eggplant

2 medium zucchini, halved lengthwise

2 yellow squash, halved lengthwise

1 yellow bell pepper, stemmed, seeded, and quartered

1 red bell pepper, stemmed, seeded, and quartered

1 loaf vegan Italian bread with a firm crust

1 ripe tomato

2 cups baby arugula

The Blue Pear

Yep, you read it correctly: blue cheese! There is indeed vegan blue cheese in the world. And it's so worth the effort to find it. If you've never tasted the sophisticated alliance of pears and blue cheese before, you're in for quite a grill thrill.

Heat the grill to medium-high.

Brush all sides of the bread slices with the olive oil. Make sandwiches with the pears sprinkled generously with the cheese. Grill for 3 to 4 minutes, turning once, until bread is browned. Drizzle the maple syrup over the pears and cheese, if desired.

YIELD: 4 sandwiches

8 slices vegan sourdough bread

¼ cup mild extra-virgin olive oil

2 ripe pears, peeled and sliced thinly

½ cup crumbled vegan blue cheese

Pure maple syrup, for drizzling (optional)

Note: If you don't have a nearby source for vegan blue cheese, you can order it online from such retailers as www.buteisland.com.

¼ cup vegan mayonnaise
(store-bought, or see pages 77
and 156)

3 cloves garlic, minced

1 tablespoon freshly squeezed
lemon juice

1 cup sliced and seeded red
bell peppers

1 medium-size zucchini, sliced

1 medium-size red onion, sliced

1 small yellow squash, sliced

¼ cup extra-virgin olive oil

Canola or vegetable oil, for brushing
the grill

2 slices vegan focaccia bread,
about 4 by 6 inches, split horizontally

Grilled Vegetables on Focaccia

Served open-faced and brimming with classic grilled vegetables, these are the perfect lunch sandwiches in the shade of an umbrella table. Especially when garnished with a round of cool cocktails (see Chapter 12 ASAP!).

In a medium-size bowl, mix the mayonnaise, garlic, and lemon juice. Set aside in the refrigerator.

In a large bowl, place the peppers, zucchini, onion, and squash slices. Stir the olive oil into the vegetables until all are coated.

Brush the grate with the canola oil. Heat the grill to medium-high. Place the pepper and zucchini slices closest to the middle of the grill, and arrange the onion and squash pieces around them. Grill for about 3 minutes, turn, and grill for 3 minutes more. Remove the vegetables from the grill and return them to the large bowl.

Place the bread on the grill and toast, turning, for about 3 minutes. Then spread some of the mayonnaise mixture on the cut sides of the focaccia and reheat on the grill, spread side up, until just heated through. Remove from the grill and layer with the vegetables. Serve as open-faced sandwiches.

YIELD: 4 servings

Broccoli Slawwiches

These grilled slaw sandwiches are a sight for hungry eyes. Melted vegan cheese, crisp bread, and crunchy homemade broccoli slaw (which can also double as a stand-alone picnic side dish) make even casual backyard meals feel as if you're getting more than your money's worth of food and fun!

Heat the grill to medium-high.

In a small bowl, combine the slaw, mayonnaise, and mustard, and mix well. Brush one side of all eight slices of bread with the olive oil and place the slices, oiled side down, on a platter. Divide the cheese among four slices of bread, then top the cheese with the slaw. Make sandwiches with the oiled sides of the bread on the outside. Grill for about 6 minutes, turning once, until the bread is nicely browned. Cut each sandwich in half and serve promptly.

YIELD: 4 sandwiches

2 cups broccoli coleslaw
(store-bought, or see recipe
that follows)

⅓ cup vegan mayonnaise
(store-bought, or see pages 77
and 156)

2 tablespoons yellow mustard

¼ cup extra-virgin olive oil

8 slices vegan cheese of choice,
or equivalent amount grated

8 slices vegan whole wheat bread

Note: Prepared broccoli coleslaw, or some approximation, is available in most supermarkets. Also, a recipe for a homemade version follows.

1 large head of purple cabbage

1½ cups broccoli florets

1 medium-size red onion, peeled

½ cup toasted sunflower seeds
(see directions for toasting on
page 52)

½ cup sugar

½ cup vegan mayonnaise
(store-bought, or see pages 77
and 156) (If serving this as a side
dish alone, make it 1 cup vegan
mayonnaise.)

1 tablespoon cider vinegar

bodacious broccoli slaw

Chop the cabbage, broccoli, and red onion into matchstick slices. In a large bowl, toss with the sunflower seeds. Just before serving, in a medium-size bowl, whisk together the sugar, mayonnaise, and vinegar. Pour over the slaw and toss to coat well.

YIELD: 6 to 8 servings

Two-Faced Avocado Sandwiches

Named after horticulturist Rudolph Hass, the avocados here prove once more how when it comes to grilling, meat-free equals scrumptious creativity. Decked out in summer's finest avocado spread and baby arugula, these open-faced sandwiches are as simple as they are exquisite, and will really give your guests something to talk about behind your back! Be prepared to make plenty, because they'll go in a snap.

In a bowl, mash the avocados with a fork. Sprinkle with the lemon juice to prevent the avocado from browning. Season the mashed avocado to taste with the oregano, thyme, salt, and pepper. Cover and set aside for ½ hour to let the flavors blend.

Heat the grill to medium-high. Lightly toast the bread on both sides, about 2 minutes. Then spread one side of each slice with the avocado mixture. Return to the grill, avocado side up, and grill for a few minutes, until the avocado mixture just starts to bubble. Remove from the grill, sprinkle with the arugula, and serve at once.

YIELD: 4 servings

2 ripe Hass avocados (see note), peeled and pitted

Juice of 1 lemon

Fresh or dried oregano

Fresh or dried thyme

Salt and freshly ground black pepper

4 slices vegan 7-grain bread

About 1 cup baby arugula leaves or watercress

Note: Ripe avocados will have noticeable "give" when you press around the stem with your index finger.

Extra-virgin olive oil, for oiling the grate and brushing the bread

1 pound extra-firm tofu, sliced into either six ¼-inch large slices or 12 strips, pressed and drained (see page 14; flavored or marinated tofu also works nicely; just eliminate the soy sauce then.)

1 tablespoon soy sauce

12 slices vegan whole wheat bread

2 tablespoons whole-grain mustard

2 tablespoons vegan mayonnaise (store-bought, or see pages 77 and 156)

6 romaine lettuce leaves, cut or folded to fit between the bread slices, or enough spinach to cover

6 ripe tomato slices

Variation: For a change, red pepper hummus is also a nice stand-in for the mustard and mayonnaise.

TLT

This reinvented take on a classic comfort sandwich is almost too pretty to eat, with its thick juicy red slices of tomato, airy green leafs of lettuce, crispy golden tofu, and grill toasted bread. Mmmmmm. I said *almost*! Dig in while it's still warm.

Oil the grate with the olive oil and then heat the grill to medium heat. Place the tofu on the oiled grate or a grilling screen for about 6 minutes, turning once or twice, or until golden. Once the tofu is finished, remove it from the grill and, if using unflavored tofu, sprinkle it with the soy sauce, turning to coat both sides.

At the same time, brush the bread slices with the olive oil on both sides. Place the slices on an upper grate or over indirect heat, toasting them to desired doneness.

Lightly spread the mustard and/or mayonnaise on the toast as desired. Top with slices of tofu, lettuce, and tomato and serve promptly. A big dill pickle on the side is always a welcome garnish.

YIELD: 6 sandwiches

Backyard PB & J

A foolproof peace offering to finicky little eaters or a decadent indulgence for your inner child, this grilled peanut butter and jelly sandwich will make everyone feel young-at-heart and carefree from the first bite. Pair a natural, vegan peanut butter with vegan jelly or jam (see note) and even toss on a few banana slices if desired, to really make your grill kid-tested, family-approved!

Heat the grill to medium.

Spread the peanut butter on one slice of the bread, and spread the jelly/jam on the other slice. If desired, add the banana slices. Put the two slices of bread together.

Brush the outside of the sandwich with the olive oil. Place the sandwich on the grill and toast for 2 to 4 minutes per side, or until golden brown.

Or, pop the sandwich into a mountain pie maker (see page 9) for a toasty warm campfire version.

YIELD: 1 serving

2 slices vegan whole wheat bread, or bread of choice

2 teaspoons to 1 tablespoon vegan peanut butter (see note)

2 teaspoons vegan jelly or jam of choice (see note)

½ banana, sliced (optional)

Vegetable or canola oil, or vegan margarine, for brushing the sandwich

Note: Most jellies contain gelatin, which is not vegan, so pay close attention to labels and lists of ingredients when shopping. Most jams, which often contain fruit pectin, are vegan. A variety of homemade vegan jelly and jam recipes can be found online. Likewise, some peanut butters contain ingredients that are not vegan, so again, be sure to read labels and ingredient lists when making your choice.

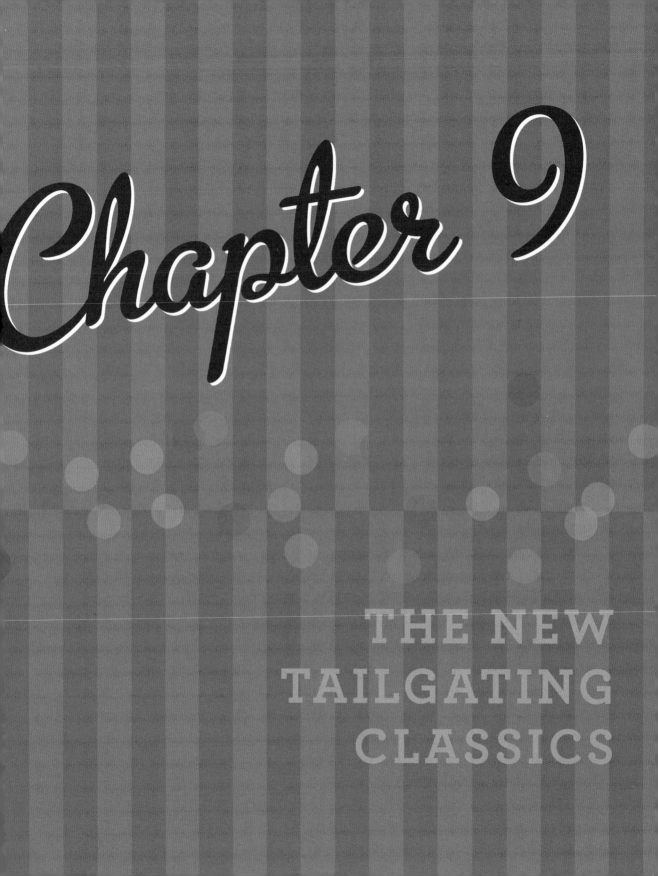

Chapter 9

THE NEW TAILGATING CLASSICS

No matter your sport of choice, tailgating is a time-honored tradition that is serious business, especially when it comes to feeding the fans.

Whether pregaming on the sidelines or while parked on the couch, you and your grill will always be ready to cheer on the home team with this roster of reinvented classics—pizza, tacos, seitan flares, jalapeño poppers, blooming onion, fries, and more. But get ready to see these favorites as never before, because going for the win grillside just became a whole new ball game.

Each of these flamed dishes plays to the sporty flavors we've grown to love, but with a charred twist, combining the best vegetables of the season and other ingredients (minus the grease) with a quick and easy turnover, leaving ample time for seconds, thirds, and plenty of armchair quarterbacking.

When you put this lineup of dishes in to play the field on game day, the fans will have only one word for you: SCORE!

1 pound slender asparagus

10 green onions, root ends trimmed, white and light green parts only

10 large shiitake mushroom caps, or large white mushroom caps

½ pound firm tofu, cubed or diced, as you prefer, pressed and drained (see page 14)

2 tablespoons extra-virgin olive oil, plus additional for brushing the toasted bread

8 roughly chopped sun-dried tomatoes, oil-packed

6 thick slices of your favorite vegan bread

Kosher salt and freshly ground black pepper

Note: Be careful during the final grilling phase here—the bread can burn easily.

Halftime Pizza with Asparagus, Mushrooms & Sun-Dried Tomatoes

Whether rooting for the home team or taking a break during a pickup game in the backyard, this easy grilled pizza made with thick slices of bread and all the trimmings scores big time in man caves, for a girls' night out, and at all friendly scrimmages.

Heat the grill to medium.

In a large bowl, combine the asparagus, green onions, mushrooms, and tofu with the olive oil and toss to mix well.

Grill, using a grilling screen if necessary, the asparagus, green onions, mushrooms, and tofu, turning every few minutes until slightly past crisp-tender. While the vegetables are grilling, place the sun-dried tomatoes in the bowl with the olive oil left behind by the vegetables. When the grilled vegetables are cool enough to handle, slice the asparagus and mushrooms into bite-size pieces, and chop the green onions. Return, along with the tofu, to the bowl with the sun-dried tomatoes.

Grill the bread lightly on one side and brush both sides lightly with the olive oil. Divide the tofu mixture among the toasted sides of the bread, return to the grill, untoasted side down and filling side up. Cover the grill and toast for about 2 minutes, making sure not to burn the undersides of the bread. You may need to move the pizzas away from the direct heat and place over indirect heat.

Cut the slices in half, season lightly with the kosher salt and pepper to taste, and serve at once.

YIELD: 6 slices

Seventh Inning Stretch Tacos

Top these sporty zucchini and mushroom tacos with a stretch of your favorite bottled salsa, perhaps stirred with some chopped cilantro to freshen it up, or some homemade Salsa Grand Slam on page 148. Some like it hot, so make sure you have all your bases covered by also chopping up a few jalapeños to pass around in a bowl.

Brush the grates with a bit of the olive oil, and heat the grill to high.

Line a baking sheet with heavy-duty aluminum foil and arrange the zucchini, mushrooms, and green onions on the foil. Drizzle with 2 to 3 tablespoons of the olive oil and season to taste with the sea salt and pepper.

Grill the vegetables, turning once, the zucchini for 8 minutes, the mushrooms for 6 minutes, and the green onions for 3 minutes.

Return the vegetables to the foil-lined sheet. Using scissors, slice the mushrooms into ½-inch strips and cut the green onions into ¼-inch pieces. Keep the vegetables warm.

Lightly brush the corn tortillas with 1 tablespoon of the olive oil, and grill them, turning often, until lightly browned but still pliable. Place two tortillas on each of four serving plates, and divide the vegetables over the tortillas. Serve at once, passing the salsa.

YIELD: 4 servings

¼ cup extra-virgin olive oil

3 medium-size zucchini, sliced into ½-inch diagonal pieces to yield larger pieces

4 portobello mushrooms, stemmed and with the black gills scraped out

10 green onions, white and light green parts only, roots sliced off

Sea salt and freshly ground black pepper

8 vegan corn tortillas

Vegan salsa of choice (see headnote; or see Salsa Grand Slam on page 148)

Salsa Grand Slam

2 tablespoons canola oil

Salt and freshly ground black pepper

4 medium-size ripe-but-still-firm tomatoes, stemmed and halved

1 medium-size red onion, skinned and halved

2 jalapeños, or more to taste, stemmed and minced

2 Anaheim chiles, stemmed and diced

Juice of 1 small lime

1 tablespoon chopped fresh cilantro leaves

Plenty of vegan tortilla chips

Get ready to knock this one out of the ballpark! Grilling fresh salsa ingredients really deepens the overall flavors of this all-time tailgating favorite. You might want to double this recipe, because it really disappears fast, especially on game day. If you dare (and I double-dog dare you!), you can raise the heat level even more by increasing the number of jalapeños and/or by adding Tabasco or another hot sauce to taste.

In a resealable plastic bag, combine the canola oil and salt and pepper to taste. Add the tomatoes and onion, and turn the bag to coat the vegetables. Marinate for 1 hour.

Heat the grill to medium. Place the onion halves on the grill grate, cut side down, and grill them until they start to brown, about 4 minutes. Add the tomatoes to the grate and grill them until their skins can be easily removed. Transfer the tomatoes and onions to a cutting board. Finely chop them, then transfer them to a large bowl and add the jalapeños, chilies, lime juice, and cilantro. Stir well, then refrigerate until just cool, or serve at room temperature with the tortilla chips.

YIELD: About 2 cups

Flame Day Fries

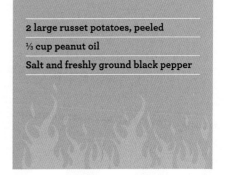

2 large russet potatoes, peeled

⅓ cup peanut oil

Salt and freshly ground black pepper

Outside of county fairs and festivals, where chowing down on greasy French fries is practically mandatory, you can now grill up a batch of fries in your own neck of the woods. Perfect for tailgating and other parties, munching on these golden glow sticks is especially decadent while afloat in a pool, playing beach bum, or when watching the night sky flicker by in the middle of nowhere.

Heat the grill to medium-high.

Slice the potatoes into long strips, about ⅓ inch thick. Transfer the sliced potatoes to a large bowl and cover with hot water. Soak the potatoes for about 10 minutes, then transfer to paper towels and thoroughly pat them dry. (Don't neglect to soak the cut potatoes in hot water. This will result in crisp fries with a creamy interior.) Place the potatoes in a large, dry bowl. Add 1 tablespoon of the oil, and salt and pepper to taste. Shake the bowl several times to toss the potatoes in the oil and seasonings.

Pour the remaining oil into a large cast-iron skillet and transfer the skillet to the hot grill. Heat the oil until it's almost smoking, then add the fries, just enough to fill the pan without crowding.

Or place the fries on an oiled grilling screen. Fry them, turning with tongs or a spatula to brown them lightly all over. Be aware that the fries grilled on a screen will lose a bit more moisture than those grilled in a skillet, so watch them extra closely.

When they're done to your liking, transfer them to a rack over paper towels to remove excess oil.

YIELD: 3 to 4 servings

1 pound seitan, torn or cut into chunks large enough to fit loosely on the grill grate, or skewered

Extra-virgin olive oil

HOT SAUCE (OR USE DROP IT LIKE IT'S HOT SAUCE ON PAGE 118)

¼ cup of your favorite hot sauce, Frank's Red Hot Cayenne Pepper Sauce preferred

3 tablespoons pure maple syrup

¼ cup freshly squeezed lime juice

½ teaspoon salt

Ground cayenne pepper (the more, the hotter!)

2 tablespoons chopped fresh oregano (optional)

Seitan Flares

If you like hot wings, I mean really, really like HOT wings, try this grilled version made with seitan! Boasting the same texture and *knock you on your ass* flavors as regular hot wings, especially when you pile on the cayenne, you won't miss a beat.

Heat the grill to medium-high.

Prepare the seitan: Marinate the seitan in the olive oil to cover for 1 hour. Grill the seitan until lightly browned, 3 to 5 minutes or longer, turning often. Transfer to a bowl.

Meanwhile, make the sauce, if using: In a glass measure, whisk together the hot sauce, maple syrup, lime juice, salt, and cayenne pepper to taste. Microwave the mixture for 1 minute or until fairly hot, or whisk the mixture together in a small saucepan and place it over direct heat on the grill until it is hot, 4 to 5 minutes, or longer depending on the grill. Add the mixture to the seitan bowl and stir gently to combine, or coat the seitan if it is skewered. Finish with the optional oregano.

Or, marinate the seitan in the Drop It like It's Hot Sauce for several hours to overnight. Arrange the seitan on skewers, if desired, and place it on the grill for 6 to 8 minutes, turning often, or until browned. Continue to brush on the hot sauce. Serve with extra sauce and celery sticks.

YIELD: 4 servings

Shiny Happy Poppers

Nothing puts a smile on people's faces faster while at the same time setting their tongues ablaze, like these grilled jalapeño poppers. Sans cheese, and debuting with a snazzy new look, these Shiny Happy Poppers are every bit a modern twist on what still remains a classic fire-brand when it comes to pregame appetizers. However, a word to the wise: Having an ice-cold beer nearby is highly recommended, should this blaze get out of control.

Heat the grill to medium-high.

Stem the jalapeños and cut one lengthwise slit in each pepper. Pull out the seeds and inner ribs with your fingers (wear rubber gloves if your skin is sensitive to handling hot peppers).

In a medium-size bowl, combine the rice, black beans, mustard, garlic powder, and thyme. Stir until well mixed.

With an appropriately sized spoon, fill the jalapeños with the rice mixture. Place the peppers on a large sheet of heavy-duty aluminum foil. Drizzle the peppers with the olive oil and then with the hot sauce, to taste.

Fold the foil into a packet with the peppers in one layer. Grill the packet for 15 to 20 minutes, or until the peppers are soft and the rice filling is hot. Serve at once.

YIELD: 1 dozen poppers

12 jalapeños

1 cup cooked white or brown rice

1 cup canned black beans, drained and rinsed

2 tablespoons smooth or grainy vegan Dijon mustard

1 teaspoon garlic powder, or 1 medium-size clove garlic, peeled and pressed

1 tablespoon chopped fresh thyme leaves, or 2 teaspoons dried

½ cup extra-virgin olive oil, for drizzling

Hot sauce of choice, for drizzling

Note: You can temper the spiciness of jalapeños—at least somewhat—by removing the seeds and especially the white inner ribs, before stuffing them with the beans and rice.

1 large white eggplant

MARINADE

3 tablespoons extra-virgin olive oil

2 tablespoons balsamic vinegar

2 teaspoons garlic powder

2 teaspoons onion powder

¼ teaspoon dried thyme

¼ teaspoon dried dill

¼ teaspoon dried oregano

1 tablespoon minced fresh basil leaves

Salt and freshly ground black pepper

Balsamic & Herb Eggplant Strips

These robust eggplant strips brushed with a lively herb vinaigrette are revved and ready to turn your grill into Victory Lane anytime you want. But consider grilling up a double or triple batch, because they have a tendency to race off the table!

Heat the grill to hot.

Prepare the eggplant: Slice the eggplant lengthwise into long ½-inch strips, trimmed to 2 to 3 inches in width.

Prepare the sauce: In a medium-size bowl, whisk together all the marinade ingredients.

Brush both sides of the eggplant strips with the vinaigrette and transfer to the hot grill. Grill for 15 to 18 minutes, turning once. Serve warm.

YIELD: About 4 servings

Blooming Onion with Sauce on the Sidelines

With or without a green thumb, this is one of nature's only creations that you can make bloom any time your little heart, or the home team, desires. For the sauce, you can choose one of your own favorites or quickly whip together some vegan mayonnaise, minced pickle, caraway, and a dash (or more!!!) of Tabasco.

Heat the grill to medium-high.

Prepare the onion: In a medium-size bowl, whisk together the canola oil, seasoned salt and white pepper to taste, and onion powder. Place the onion on a plate, cut side up, and pour the oil mixture over it. Grill the onion, cut side down, over direct heat until pliable and soft, about 20 minutes. If desired, grill the onion, cut side up, for 3 to 5 minutes at the end.

Meanwhile, make the sauce. In a medium-size bowl, whisk together all the sauce ingredients. Divide the dipping sauce among four ramekins.

Cut the onion into four serving pieces and serve with the homemade dipping sauce or other sauce of choice.

YIELD: 4 servings

BLOOMING ONION

2 tablespoons canola oil

Seasoned salt, such as Lawry's

Freshly ground white pepper

2 teaspoons onion powder

1 large onion, peeled and sliced into "petals" most of the way through, leaving the stem end intact (see note)

SAUCE ON THE SIDELINES

1 cup vegan mayonnaise (store-bought, or see pages 77 and 156)

2 tablespoons minced sweet or dill pickle

1 teaspoon finely ground caraway seeds

Dash of Tabasco sauce, or more to taste

Note: If you happen to have one of those "blooming onion" cutting contraptions, by all means use it, but lower the grilling time a bit. Also, use a Vidalia onion if you want a sweeter flavor.

CORN

2 tablespoons corn oil

¾ teaspoon chili powder

¼ teaspoon salt

4 ears corn, husked or see husked alternative

PIQUANT SAUCE

¼ cup vegan mayonnaise (store-bought, or see recipe that follows)

3 tablespoons chopped fresh cilantro

1 clove garlic, peeled and pressed or finely chopped

¼ teaspoon freshly ground black pepper

¼ teaspoon cayenne pepper

4 teaspoons freshly squeezed lime juice, from about ½ lime

HOMEMADE RED VEGAN MAYONNAISE

3 tablespoons freshly squeezed lemon or lime juice

½ cup soy milk

½ teaspoon salt

¼ teaspoon Hungarian or smoked Spanish paprika

¼ teaspoon dry mustard

⅓ cup canola oil

Grilled Corn on the Cob with Piquant Sauce

Knee-high by the Fourth of July means, soon after, you'll be tailgating your way down rows of juicy yellow kernels grilled and dripping with a totally rad cilantro, garlic, and cayenne-infused sauce. BTW, *piquant* is really just another word for rowdy, which is really just another way of saying FUN FUN FUN!

Heat the grill to medium-high.

Prepare the corn: In a small bowl, whisk together the corn oil, chili powder, and salt. Rub the corn all over with the mixture. Wrap the corn in aluminum foil and grill it, turning often with tongs, for about 25 minutes. Remove the foil and finish grilling right on the grates, about 5 minutes. Or peel back the husks, remove the silk, season the corn, then pull the husks back over the kernels before grilling for a nice smoky flavor.

Meanwhile, make the sauce. In a medium-size bowl, combine all the sauce ingredients. Slather the grilled corn with the mayonnaise mixture and serve at once.

YIELD: 4 ears corn

homemade red vegan mayonnaise

In a blender, combine the lemon juice, soy milk, salt, paprika, and mustard powder. Blend on low speed, then very slowly add the canola oil until the mixture thickens, 1 to 2 minutes. Transfer the mayonnaise to a sealable jar and keep refrigerated, where it will last for 3 to 4 days.

YIELD: ¾ cup

Chapter 10

SUPPER UNDER THE STARS

Whether by surf or turf, your grill has you covered. When entertaining at suppertime, these main dishes can run from swimsuit casual to sundress and chinos chic, or romantic dinner for two to flash mob cookout.

Layering complementary flavors and striking that perfect balance of ingredients is particularly evident in these showstoppers, which will appeal to cravings for down-home cuisine as well as inspired take-offs of popular Mexican, Italian, and Asian dishes. For starters, this chapter debuts the amazing grilled spaghetti squash, which will catch the eye of young and old alike, especially when topped with a toothsome tomato, black bean, and zucchini medley. Meanwhile, the flame-kissed Veggie Quesadillas, Zucchinicotti, and a multilevel no-bake lasagne demonstrate how literally building a main course with grilled vegetables, spices, and herbs can result in an explosion of flavors, including tasty exclamation points such as Sparky Corn Relish and Toasted Pine Nut Pesto.

Tempeh also shines here in three mouthwatering entrées, demonstrating again why this hearty meat analogue was practically custom-made for the grill. The Maple-Soy Tempeh over Rice and Tex-Mex Tempeh for Two both easily achieve charred "grate"-ness. And, if you thought the words *steak on the grill* would never again pass your lips, get ready for Tempeh Steaks on the Grill bathed in a spirited rice wine marinade.

I also have you covered for a laid-back pizza night or a more upscale affair featuring the Starry Night Tart, both designed to blow your mind!

1 medium large spaghetti squash (about 2 pounds)

2 zucchini, sliced lengthwise into ¼-inch thick slices

Extra-virgin olive oil, for brushing, plus 2 tablespoons

2 cups chopped peeled and seeded tomatoes, or 1 (14-ounce) can diced tomatoes

1 (14-ounce) can black beans, drained and rinsed

8 fresh basil leaves, julienned

2 tablespoons red wine vinegar

1 teaspoon garlic powder

½ teaspoon salt

Roasted Spaghetti Squash with Tomatoes, Back Beans & Zucchini

Spaghetti squash, or vegetable spaghetti, brings out the kid in all of us. A spectacular stand-in for pasta, the grilled spaghetti squash here is topped with a seasoned combo that will really cinch its claim to flame.

Heat the grill to medium.

With a sharp fork, pierce the squash in several places. Wrap the squash loosely in heavy-duty aluminum foil. Roast the squash in the covered grill for about an hour, or until it "gives" when pressed with a spoon, turning a quarter-turn every 15 minutes. Remove from the grill and let the squash stand in the foil for 15 minutes.

While the spaghetti squash stands, rub the zucchini with the olive oil and grill it over medium heat, uncovered, for 4 minutes or until tender, turning once. Remove from the grill and slice into bite-size pieces.

When the squash has rested for 15 minutes, remove it from the foil and cut it in half. Scoop out the seeds and, using two forks, scrape the squash flesh into strands and transfer to a large bowl.

In a medium-size bowl, combine the tomatoes, beans, zucchini, and basil.

In a small bowl, combine the remaining 2 tablespoons of olive oil with the vinegar, garlic powder, and salt, and stir with a fork to blend thoroughly. Pour this over the tomato mixture and toss to combine. Top the spaghetti squash with the mixture, and serve.

YIELD: 4 servings

1 medium-size zucchini, cut lengthwise into ¼-inch strips

1 yellow squash, cut lengthwise into ¼-inch strips

1 small red onion, cut into ¼-inch slices

1 medium-size red bell pepper, stemmed, seeded, and cut into ½-inch strips

Extra-virgin olive or canola oil, for brushing

2 ounces vegan cream cheese, at room temperature (see note)

Juice of ½ lime

2 to 3 pinches of ground cumin

Hot pepper sauce

8 (6-inch) vegan corn tortillas

Sparky Corn Relish (recipe follows)

Note: If you do not have a nearby source for vegan cream cheese, it is available online at www.tofutti.com and www.followyourheart.com.

Veggie Quesadillas with Sparky Corn Relish

The homemade corn relish, with cider vinegar, Dijon mustard, turmeric, and more, galvanizes these grilled veggie tortillas. Also, it should come as no surprise by now that I like to be pretty liberal with the hot pepper sauce for an added sizzle factor, if you care to join me.

Heat the grill to medium-high.

Brush the zucchini, squash, onion, and bell pepper with the olive oil and then grill for 3 to 4 minutes, or until tender. Transfer to a cutting board and cut into bite-size pieces with kitchen shears.

Meanwhile, in a medium-size bowl, combine the cream cheese, lime juice, cumin, and hot pepper sauce to taste. Add the vegetable pieces and stir to combine.

Toast the tortillas on the hot grill, 20 to 30 seconds per side, or until lightly browned and pliable.

Spread ⅓ cup of the vegetable mixture over four of the tortillas. Cover with the remaining four tortillas and press lightly.

Serve at once with the corn relish.

YIELD: 4 filled tortillas

sparky corn relish

In a medium-size saucepan, combine the vinegar, sugar, mustard, and turmeric. Bring to a slow boil over medium heat. Add the corn, onion, and bell pepper and simmer for 5 minutes. Serve hot, cold, or at room temperature.

YIELD: 1½ cups

⅓ cup cider vinegar

½ cup sugar

1 teaspoon vegan Dijon mustard

¼ teaspoon turmeric

1½ cups corn kernels, frozen or fresh

¼ cup diced red onion

¼ cup diced and seeded red and green bell pepper

Presto Pesto No-Bake Lasagne

Grilling and lasagne! These are two concepts most people are not used to seeing together, but here we break all the conventional rules, proving that when it comes to our favorite food and a grill, anything is possible.

Prepare the marinade: In a medium-size saucepan over medium-high stovetop heat, heat the olive oil, lemon zest, garlic powder, and onion powder. When the mixture begins to bubble, remove from the heat and let cool. When the mixture is at room temperature, stir in the lemon juice, and season to taste with the salt and white pepper.

Meanwhile, make the pesto: In a mini-processor, puree the pine nuts. Add the garlic powder and basil leaves, and pulse until well combined. Pour in the olive oil and pulse until pureed. Season to taste with the salt and white pepper.

Heat the grill to medium.

Prepare the lasagne: Brush the zucchini and squash slices with the olive oil, and season to taste with salt and pepper. Grill the slices until slightly charred, 8 minutes, turning once. Transfer to a bowl and drizzle with about half of the marinade.

Grill the tofu slices about 3 minutes per side, then let cool slightly before slicing into 1/8-inch-thick pieces.

Place three slices of zucchini and three slices of squash, alternating slices, on a platter to form a 6 by 8-inch rectangle. Spread 3 tablespoons of the pesto over the slices. Top with a layer of the spinach. Cover with a 6 by 8-inch layer of the tofu. Top with a layer of tomatoes and season with half the oregano, and salt and pepper to taste. Finish with six to eight basil leaves. Repeat the layering. Carve into squares and serve at room temperature.

YIELD: 4 to 6 servings

OLIVE OIL & LEMON MARINADE

¾ cup extra-virgin olive oil

1 teaspoon grated lemon zest

3 teaspoons garlic powder

2 teaspoons onion powder

Juice of 2 lemons

Salt and freshly ground white pepper

TOASTED PINE NUT PESTO

½ cup toasted pine nuts (see toasting directions on page 52)

1 teaspoon garlic powder

2 cups fresh basil leaves

½ cup extra-virgin olive oil

Salt and freshly ground white pepper

LASAGNE

5 zucchini and yellow squash (mix and match as desired), stemmed, trimmed, and sliced lengthwise into ¼-inch slices

Extra-virgin olive oil, for brushing

Salt and freshly ground white pepper

12 to 14 ounces extra-firm tofu, cut into 1-inch slices, pressed and drained (see page 14)

1 cup cooked, chopped spinach

2 medium-size ripe tomatoes, cut into ¼-inch slices

3 teaspoons dried oregano

18 basil leaves

12 dried manicotti tubes

1 medium-size red onion, cut into
½-inch slices

4 zucchini, trimmed and quartered
lengthwise

2 tablespoons extra-virgin olive oil

2 teaspoons garlic powder

1½ cups chopped vegan cream cheese
(see note)

Salt and freshly ground black pepper

1 (14-ounce) can diced organic
tomatoes

1 cup vegan Parmesan cheese
(store-bought or see recipe
that follows)

*Note: If you do not have a nearby source
for vegan cream cheese, it is available
online at www.tofutti.com and www.follow
yourheart.com.*

HOMEMADE VEGAN PARMESAN CHEESE

1 cup slivered almonds

5 tablespoons nutritional yeast

1 teaspoon lemon zest

Salt and freshly ground white pepper

Zucchinicotti

The grill has its own plans for this Italian-inspired favorite. Stuffed with a grill-revved zucchini and onion
mixture, this fabulous overhaul of traditional manicotti
turns every meal into exactly what it should be: a special
occasion.

Cook the manicotti tubes until al dente according to the manufacturer's instructions.

Heat the grill to medium-low.

Brush the onion and zucchini slices with the olive oil, then
grill them until the zucchini is tender, 8 to 10 minutes, turning
occasionally. Cool the onion and zucchini, then combine with
the garlic powder and cream cheese. Mix well, and add the salt
and pepper to taste.

Preheat oven to 350°F. Stuff the manicotti tubes with the zucchini mixture and arrange in a 9 by 13-inch baking pan. Pour
the diced tomatoes over the tubes. Cover with foil and bake for
25 to 30 minutes. Uncover, sprinkle with the remaining cream
cheese and Parmesan cheese, and bake for 10 minutes longer.
Serve after a 5-minute rest.

YIELD: 4 to 6 servings

homemade vegan parmesan cheese

In a blender or mini-processor, combine all the ingredients.
Pulse until the ingredients form crumbs the size of a half-
grain of rice. This mixture can be stored in the refrigerator
for 3 to 4 days.

YIELD: About 1⅓ cups

Grilled Picnic Pizza

Yes, not only can your grill give you amazing lasagne and manicotti, but pizza, too. By the time the moon hits your eye, you'll be feasting on a big-a pizza pie, compliments of your grill! Switch things up for your next barbecue by turning it into a pizza party where you get to run wild with the toppings. Also, the quick prep will let you turn out several grill-striped pizzas, if needed, even varying the toppings to suit all your guests' tastes.

Create zones of direct (medium heat) and indirect heat on your grill (see page 10). Slice as desired the toppings you choose, brush them with the olive oil, and grill them to your preferred level of tenderness. Keep them warm while grilling the pizza crust.

Generously brush both sides of the pizza crust with the olive oil. Place the crust over direct heat for 1 to 2 minutes, or until the bottom is lightly browned and the top begins to get very warm. (Grilling times may vary based on the thickness of the crust.) Transfer the crust to indirect heat for 4 to 6 minutes, or until the bottom is browned and crispy. Turn over the crust and place the uncooked side over the direct heat for 1 to 2 minutes, until lightly browned. Transfer to indirect heat. Top with the grilled and/or ungrilled toppings of choice and the herbs, and return the pizza to direct heat for 4 to 6 minutes, or until the pizza reaches the desired doneness.

Or place the oiled pizza crust with toppings on a pizza stone set over direct heat, and grill until the pizza is browned and crispy as desired. Of course, by cooking the pizza this way, you will be forfeiting the grill marks.

YIELD: 1 pizza

Your choice of grilled and/or ungrilled toppings:
  Mushrooms
  Onions
  Garlic
  Bell pepper
  Tomato slices
  Broccoli
  Zucchini
  Sautéed spinach
  Fresh arugula leaves
  Banana peppers
  Jalapeños
  Nutritional yeast

Extra-virgin olive oil

1 prebaked thin vegan pizza crust

1 teaspoon finely chopped fresh rosemary leaves

½ teaspoon crushed dried red pepper flakes

1 teaspoon dried oregano

1 tablespoon minced fresh basil, if using tomatoes

Note: The overachievers out there may want to make their own pizza crust, which is fine by me (there are many vegan pizza crust recipes online), but for our purposes here, my goal is to get the party started as soon as possible, so this recipe calls for a prebaked vegan crust, which is pretty widely available in stores and online. That simply means read labels and ingredient lists when shopping for the crust.

1 (8-ounce) package tempeh

3 tablespoons pure maple syrup

3 tablespoons soy sauce

1 teaspoon rice wine vinegar

1 teaspoon rice wine

1 teaspoon molasses

2 cloves garlic, peeled and pressed
or chopped finely

¼ teaspoon cayenne pepper

2 portobello mushroom caps,
black gills scraped away

2½ cups cooked brown rice,
still warm

1 cup blanched broccoli florets

Maple-Soy Tempeh
over Rice

When marinated tempeh, portobellos, and broccoli top off a knoll of brown rice, you and your guests will taste the glory only a grill can impart. For this splendid feast, maple syrup and soy sauce blend well, and give a nice background flavor to the ever-accommodating tempeh.

Slice the tempeh diagonally into four triangles. In a medium-size bowl, whisk together the maple syrup, soy sauce, rice vinegar, rice wine, molasses, garlic, and cayenne pepper. Reserve 2 tablespoons of the mixture to garnish the grilled tempeh.

Place the tempeh in a resealable plastic bag and pour in the marinade, reserving 2 tablespoons to garnish the grilled tempeh. Turn the bag to coat the tempeh completely, then refrigerate for at least 1 hour or up to 24 hours, turning the bag from time to time.

Remove the tempeh from the marinade and pour the marinade into another bowl. Heat the grill to medium-high and grill the tempeh for 3 minutes on each side, or longer, brushing continuously with the marinade.

Meanwhile, grill the portobello mushroom caps next to the tempeh, brushing them with some of the marinade as well.

When the tempeh has turned a deep brown and the mushrooms are browned and softened, remove and slice the tempeh and mushrooms into ½-inch strips.

Serve warm over a bed of brown rice and top with the broccoli florets. Drizzle the reserved marinade over all.

YIELD: 4 servings

3 tablespoons freshly squeezed lime juice

2 tablespoons extra-virgin olive oil

2 tablespoons soy sauce (tamari preferred)

1 tablespoon chili powder

2 cloves garlic, chopped finely

1½ teaspoons dried oregano

¼ teaspoon ground cloves

1 tablespoon adobo (from a can of chipotles in adobo), or your favorite

vegan salsa (store-bought or see Salsa Grand Slam on page 148)

1 (8-ounce) package tempeh, cut into 1-inch-thick slices

Canola oil, for oiling the grill grates

Tex-Mex Tempeh for Two

For all those candlelit fiestas for two, lime juice and spices mingle nicely to create a remarkable marinade for grilled tempeh. Heat things up even more by serving the tempeh with taco fixings, or alongside a heaping platter of flame-kissed vegetables to really turn this dish into a hunk, a hunk of burning love!

In a wide, shallow dish, whisk together the lime juice, olive oil, soy sauce, chili powder, garlic, oregano, cloves, and adobo. Arrange the tempeh in the dish, turn to coat all over with the marinade, cover and chill, turning halfway through, for 2 hours or overnight.

Grease the grates with the canola oil, then preheat the grill to medium. Grill the tempeh, flipping it once, until browned and hot throughout, 8 to 10 minutes total. Transfer to plates and serve.

YIELD: 2 servings

Tempeh Steaks on the Grill

Once more, you can toss steaks on the grill, and feel good about it. After pampering this burly tempeh in a rich, soothing marinade of rice wine vinegar, soy sauce, garlic, fresh ginger, and molasses for at least 24 hours, the pièce de résistance will come together in minutes at mealtime.

Prepare the tempeh: Score the tempeh on both sides in a crosshatch pattern, making shallow cuts about ¼ inch apart. Cut the tempeh into six portions and spread them out on a glass baking dish.

Prepare the marinade: In a medium-size bowl, whisk together all the marinade ingredients. Pour the marinade over the tempeh, turning to coat the tempeh well. Marinate the tempeh, covered and refrigerated, for at least 24 hours, turning the tempeh every so often.

Heat the grill to medium-high. Grill the tempeh for 6 minutes on each side. Transfer to four to six plates and garnish with the green onion slivers.

YIELD: 4 to 6 servings

3 pounds tempeh

2 green onions, cut into 1-inch lengths and slivered lengthwise, for garnish

MARINADE

⅓ cup rice wine vinegar

2 tablespoons rice wine

⅓ cup soy sauce

2 tablespoons water

3 cloves garlic, peeled and pressed

1-inch piece fresh ginger, peeled and minced

2 tablespoons Chinese five-spice powder, possibly a bit more

¼ cup extra-virgin olive oil

2 tablespoons molasses

Freshly ground black pepper

Ingredients

2 (14-ounce) blocks extra-firm tofu

2 cups chipotle marinade
(recipe follows)

3 medium-size zucchini, sliced into
1-inch pieces

1 red bell pepper, stemmed, seeded,
and cut into 1-inch chunks

1 medium-size red onion, sliced
into 1-inch wedges

12 cherry or pear tomatoes

Canola oil, for oiling the grill

CHIPOTLE MARINADE

1 cup vegan vegetable broth

1 clove garlic, minced

⅓ cup brown sugar

¼ cup soy sauce

3 tablespoons dry sherry

1 canned chipotle in adobo sauce,
minced

2 tablespoons adobo sauce
(from the chipotle can)

2 teaspoons onion powder

1 tablespoon smooth vegan
Dijon mustard

2 tablespoons minced fresh
cilantro leaves

Chipotle-Marinated Tofu & Vegetable Kebabs

A deliciously peculiar assortment of flavors for sure, the homemade chipotle chile marinade used for this kebab dish really turns up the heat with some searing notes that you don't generally associate with tofu, zucchini, red bell pepper, red onion, and cherry tomatoes. But now you'll always associate them with a rousing good time!

Slice each block of tofu in half and slice each half twice vertically and twice horizontally to make three dozen tofu cubes, each about an inch square. Press and drain the cubes (see page 14).

Place the tofu cubes in a resealable plastic bag, and pour the Chipotle Marinade over them. Seal the bag, place in a bowl, and marinate for 2 to 24 hours, turning the bag every so often.

Oil the grill grate with the canola oil, and then heat the grill to medium. Soak some bamboo skewers in water for at least 20 to 30 minutes. Thread the tofu, zucchini, bell pepper, red onion, and cherry tomatoes alternately onto the skewers. Place the loaded skewers on the oiled racks and grill for about 10 minutes, turning once. Don't let the vegetables burn.

YIELD: Varies with the length of the skewers, but count on at least 4 servings

chipotle marinade

In a medium-size bowl, whisk together all the ingredients.

YIELD: About 2 cups

Zucchini, Squash & Mushroom Kebabs

You'll always feel relaxed and ready at suppertime, as the ingredients for these tofu and vegetable kebabs need only 1 to 4 hours simple marinating. Red onions, zucchini, summer squash, cremini mushrooms, and tofu are soaked in an effortless and richly seasoned olive oil mixture, making this a great weeknight entrée that will easily appeal to palates up and down the picnic table.

Prepare the marinade: In a medium-size bowl, whisk the olive oil with the lime juice, salt, pepper, oregano, garlic powder, and onion powder.

Prepare the kebabs: Place the red onions, zucchini, yellow squash, mushrooms, and tofu cubes in a resealable plastic bag. Pour the olive oil marinade into the bag, place the bag in a bowl, and marinate, refrigerated, for 1 to 4 hours, turning the bag a few times.

Heat the grill to medium-high.

Thread the vegetables and tofu cubes onto skewers (presoak the skewers in water for 20 to 30 minutes if using bamboo), alternating as you see fit, leaving a little space between the vegetables so that heat can circulate. Grill until the vegetables are golden and tender, about 20 minutes, turning often. Serve warm.

YIELD: About 4 servings

MARINADE

½ cup extra-virgin olive oil

¼ cup freshly squeezed lime juice

2 teaspoons kosher salt

1 teaspoon freshly ground black pepper

2 teaspoons dried oregano

2 teaspoons garlic powder

1 teaspoon onion powder

KEBABS

4 medium-size red onions, quartered

2 medium-size zucchini, sliced into 1-inch rounds

2 medium-size yellow summer squash, sliced into 1-inch rounds

12 cremini mushrooms

1 (14-ounce) block extra-firm tofu, cut into 1-inch cubes, pressed and drained (see page 14)

Starry Night Tart with Grilled Eggplant, Zucchini & Plum Tomatoes

You may never have imagined serving a tart—*a tart!*—grillside, but now you can, thanks to this sizzling collective of eggplant, red bell pepper, zucchini, tomatoes, and seasonings. Picture this: a warm night, a long picnic table covered in a checkered cloth, a row of candles, family and friends laughing, cocktails flowing, and only the stars watching from above. Enter this divine vegetable tart fresh from the garden, hot off the grill. In other words, it's time to tell reality to take a hike.

Heat the grill to medium-high.

In a large bowl, combine the eggplant, bell pepper, zucchini, plum tomatoes, 3 tablespoons of the olive oil, garlic, salt, and pepper, mixing to coat. Separate out the eggplant and bell pepper from the zucchini and tomatoes. Bring the vegetables over to the grill. Grill the eggplant and bell pepper for 15 minutes, turning once, then put the zucchini and tomatoes on the grill, cut side down. Grill for 10 to 15 minutes, turning everything once or twice. Remove from the grill and slice all the vegetables into bite-size pieces.

Heat the oven to 450°F. On a lightly floured surface, roll the pie pastry into a 13-inch circle. Sprinkle cornmeal over a greased 14-inch circular pan, and transfer the pastry to the prepared pan.

Spoon the grilled vegetables over the pastry to within 1½ inches of the edges. Fold up the edges of pastry over the filling, leaving the center uncovered. Brush the pastry with the remaining tablespoon of olive oil.

Bake the tart for 20 to 25 minutes, or until the crust is golden brown. Sprinkle with the Parmesan and basil, and serve.

YIELD: 4 servings

1 small eggplant, halved lengthwise

1 medium-size red bell pepper, stemmed, seeded, and sliced lengthwise into 2-inch strips

1 large zucchini, halved lengthwise

4 plum tomatoes, halved lengthwise

4 tablespoons extra-virgin olive oil

4 cloves garlic, peeled and pressed

½ teaspoon salt

⅛ teaspoon freshly ground pepper

1 sheet refrigerated vegan pie pastry or puff pastry (see note)

1 tablespoon cornmeal

2 tablespoons shredded vegan Parmesan cheese (store-bought, or see page 166)

Minced fresh basil, for garnish (optional)

Note: Most commercially available refrigerated pie pastry doughs are vegan. It's actually more difficult—and more expensive—to find pie pastry made with dairy butter.

Note: One other option for preparing this tart: Bake the tart in a fluted tart pan for visual interest. And keep four additional grilled tomato halves intact for styling.

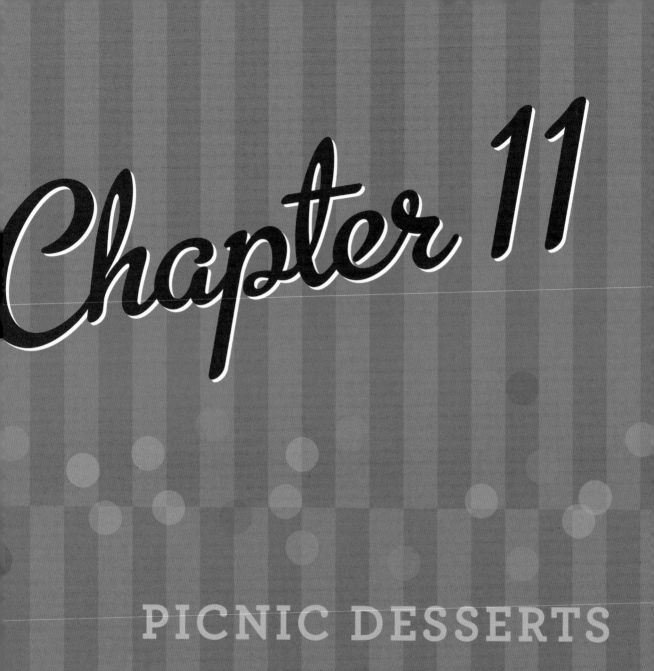

Chapter 11

PICNIC DESSERTS

If the grill has taught us anything, it is to expect the unexpected! Just when you thought the grill could not possibly transcend any other barriers of culinary convention, here comes a collection of flamed desserts that will be heralded as much for their sweet satisfaction as for their charred moxie and convenience. Grilled smokiness counters and complements the traditional sweetness of these desserts without overpowering them. A gentle kiss of flame completes their flavor profiles in a most unique way and takes them from traditional and expected to thoroughly modern and surprising.

This is where fruit and an array of other ingredients step up to the challenge and use the grill to produce a memorable finale to any meal, or standalone snacks that you can savor anytime. Cantaloupe's smooth taste is energized when it meets fire for the first time; juicy, flamed peaches play well with an unforgettably sweet raspberry sauce; and skewers full of strawberries, apples, kiwis, bananas, pineapple, papaya, and more turn the grill into a tropical island just waiting for your arrival.

The recipes that follow may just be the best excuse yet for eating your dessert first. With a tipsy cameo by Vanilla, I Scream!, campfire classics such as apple and cherry mountain pies and s'mores (!!!), chocolate-dipped coconut, and even a grill-striped vanilla pound cake with lemon-lime glaze to round out the chapter, every mouthful of these desserts is transformed into a much-deserved vacay without you ever having to leave home.

¼ cup freshly squeezed lime juice

2 tablespoons sugar

2 teaspoons minced, peeled fresh ginger

1 tablespoon minced fresh mint leaves

1 ripe cantaloupe, peeled and carved into 2-inch cubes

Grilled Cantaloupe with Fresh Ginger & Mint Leaves

It doesn't occur to many people to cook cantaloupe, let alone grill it, but the result is deliciously smoky while the lush melon flavors are ever deepened. This is a recipe you'll want to repeat several times during melon season, if you're lucky enough to find these sunny sweet orbs.

In a large bowl, combine the lemon juice, sugar, ginger, and mint. Add the cantaloupe slices and toss to coat the melon thoroughly. Let the melon mixture stand for 5 minutes at room (or outdoor) temperature.

Heat the grill to medium-high. Thread the cantaloupe pieces onto skewers. Place the skewers on the grill and cook for about 3 minutes, or until slightly soft and beginning to brown. Remove promptly from the grill and serve.

YIELD: 4 servings

Fruity Kebabs Brushed with Brown Sugar, Cinnamon & Mint

A terrific high-summer hit, to be sure! These Cointreau-splashed fruit kebabs flaunt some of nature's greatest gifts to the human palate: apples, bananas, peaches, kiwis, pineapple, and strawberries. Behold these shameless show-offs.

Heat the grill to medium.

In a small bowl, combine the vegetable oil, brown sugar, lime juice, cinnamon, and mint. Mix well with a fork until the sugar is dissolved.

If you are using bamboo skewers, be sure to soak them in water for 20 to 30 minutes to prevent them from burning.

Thread the fruit pieces onto the skewers, alternating the fruit as you wish. Brush the fruit kebabs with the sugar mixture and place them on the grill. Cook for about 7 minutes, turning frequently, until the fruit starts to brown and is heated through.

Off heat, splash the skewers with the Cointreau or brandy and serve at once.

YIELD: 4 servings

2 tablespoons vegetable oil

2 tablespoons brown sugar

2 tablespoons freshly squeezed lime juice

1 teaspoon ground cinnamon

¼ cup chopped fresh mint leaves

Juice of 1 lemon

2 apples, cored and cut into 1-inch pieces, tossed in a bowl with the lemon juice to prevent browning

2 bananas, peeled and cut into 1-inch chunks

2 peaches, pitted and cut into 1-inch slices

4 kiwis, peeled and sliced into 1-inch sections

4 (1-inch thick) slices fresh pineapple, peeled, cored, and cut into 1-inch pieces; or 1 (8-ounce) can pineapple chunks, drained

16 strawberries, washed and stemmed

Cointreau or brandy, for splashing the cooked fruit kebabs (optional, but encouraged!)

2 tablespoons sugar

1 teaspoon molasses

2 tablespoons freshly squeezed lime or lemon juice

1 cup fresh raspberries

5 medium-size unpeeled fresh peaches, halved and pitted

Nonstick vegetable oil spray, for the grill grates

Grilled Peaches with Raspberry Sauce

Instead of reading some lengthy headnote where the author uses clever verbiage and the quirky turn of a phrase to express how with a little attention peaches shine on the grill or just how out-of-this-world, off-the-hook, sinfully palatable this easy and *amaaaaaazing* dessert with a homemade raspberry sauce is, simply reread the recipe title, study it, absorb it, and devour it. After all, those five words up there say it all: YUM!

In a shallow dish, combine the sugar, molasses, and lime juice, mixing well. Add half of the raspberries and mash. Add the peach halves, turning to coat. Marinate at room temperature, cut side down, for 30 to 60 minutes.

Coat the grill rack with the vegetable oil spray and heat the grill to medium-hot. Place the peaches on the grill, cut side down. Reserve the marinade.

Turn the peaches over after 2 minutes, then cook for another 6 to 8 minutes, or until tender, basting once with half of the reserved marinade. Then remove them from the grill.

Stir the remaining raspberries into the remaining marinade and spoon over the peach halves.

Serve warm.

YIELD: 5 servings, 2 peach halves per person

CAKE

¼ cup plus 2 tablespoons canola oil

5 ounces silken soft tofu, pressed and drained (see page 14)

⅔ cup sugar

¼ cup vanilla soy milk

1 tablespoon vanilla extract

1½ cups cake flour

1½ teaspoons baking powder

1 teaspoon baking soda

½ teaspoon salt

Extra-virgin olive oil, for brushing the cake

LEMON-LIME GLAZE

½ cup powdered (confectioners') sugar

2 teaspoons freshly squeezed lime juice

2 teaspoons freshly squeezed lemon juice

2 teaspoons brandy or cognac

Pinch salt

Vanilla Pound Cake with Lemon-Lime Glaze

This dense vanilla cake can be served with or without the Lemon-Lime Glaze. In fact, it can be served with or without dinner. A showstopper through and through, this robust dessert has more than earned its grill stripes.

Preheat the oven to 350°F and heat the grill to medium-high.

Prepare the cake: Place the 2 tablespoons of canola oil in a 9 by 5-inch loaf pan and rub it around with a paper towel to coat.

In a food processor, blend the tofu, sugar, the remaining ¼ cup of the canola oil, and the soy milk and vanilla until smooth.

In a large bowl, whisk together the cake flour, baking powder, baking soda, and salt. With a rubber spatula, fold the tofu mixture into the dry ingredients, blending well. Pour the mixture into the prepared loaf pan, transfer to the hot oven, and bake for 20 minutes.

Then, transfer the loaf pan to the hot grill, cover, and grill for 10 to 15 minutes, or until a toothpick inserted into the center comes out clean. Let the cake cool for 10 minutes in the pan, then run a knife around the pan between the cake and the pan and unmold the cake. Let the cake cool on a wire rack until barely warm.

After the cake has cooled, lightly brush it with olive oil and transfer it back to the grill and toast it all over, turning as desired as the grill marks develop, 2 to 3 minutes per side, or less if the grill is still really hot.

Meanwhile, prepare the glaze. In a small bowl, whisk together all the glaze ingredients. Drizzle the glaze over the top of the cake (after it's removed from the grill) and spread with an offset spatula. Cool the cake completely before serving.

YIELD: 6 servings

Chocolate-Dipped Coconut Islands

For your next backyard luau or midnight snack, rekindle a romance that's practically as old as time itself. These sweet, grilled islands are gloriously deserted, except for a population of two: You and chocolate.

Heat the grill to medium.

Wrap the coconut in a towel and crack it open with a hammer. With a cleaver, slice the coconut into wedges and place the coconut wedges, shell side up, white sides down, on the grill grate. Grill until the white sides are lightly browned, 10 to 15 minutes, turning as needed; timing will vary according to the size of the pieces and the heat, so stick close by these tropical gems.

Carefully cut or scrape the browned coconut off the shell. Dip the browned coconut islands into the vegan chocolate, if using.

YIELD: 4 servings

1 fresh coconut (see note)

Melted vegan chocolate (optional) (see note)

Note: Picking a good coconut isn't really rocket science. It should feel fairly heavy for its size. Shake the coconut, and you should hear or feel liquid sloshing around inside. Don't select a coconut that has any liquid leaking out of the three black "eyes" at the top. Take your time cutting the coconut away from the shell. It can be dangerous working the coconut over with a knife.

Note: If you don't have a nearby source for vegan chocolate, it's available online at www.veganessentials.com.

S'More Is Always Better!

A round of "Kumbaya," anyone? Even when campfire is swapped for grill, these iconic outdoor sweet treats are still the ultimate, undefeated crowd pleaser, intoning *young hearts, be free tonight* with every ooey-gooey mouthful!

Heat the grill to medium. Prepare four 12-inch-square sheets of heavy-duty aluminum foil.

Place a graham cracker half at the center of a sheet of foil. Divide the chopped chocolate or chocolate squares among the four graham crackers. Place a marshmallow on each chocolate layer. Cover with the remaining cracker halves.

Bring the foil sides up and around each stack, then double-fold the top and both ends to seal each packet. Don't seal too tightly.

Place each packet on the grill. Cover the grill and cook for 4 to 5 minutes. Carefully open one of the packets after 4 minutes to see if the marshmallow has melted, as it should. Serve at once.

Or, go traditional, using a long stick to toast the marshmallows over a campfire until golden brown (or charred, if your prefer), and then build your s'more from there.

YIELD: 4 s'mores

4 whole vegan graham crackers, broken in half

½ cup chopped vegan chocolate or 4 thin squares of vegan chocolate

4 vegan marshmallows

Note: While vegan s'mores take a little advance planning, they are so worth it. Vegan marshmallows, which don't contain gelatin, are available at www.sweetand-sara.com, among other sites. And the best part is they react to flame just as regular marshmallows do, tanning and even charring, if desired. Sweet & Sara also offers vegan graham crackers. Vegan chocolate is widely available, including online at www.veganessentials.com.

2 slices vegan bread

Vegan margarine

Filling of choice (recipes follow for cherry and apple fillings)

Mountain Pies Around the Campfire

These first cousins to traditional grilled fare are much more fun and quicker to make than regular pie, and can yield mini sweet treats or even pizza pockets in minutes, while you get to enjoy an open fire in the great outdoors. And if you don't yet have a mountain pie maker, it's time to get one (see page 9). Consisting of a heavy cast-iron shell that's perfect for holding two slices of bread with filling and long steel handles with wooden grips, mountain pie makers take advantage of the direct heat from a glowing campfire to seal the deal with more flavor than even a hot oven.

To make 1 mountain pie: Coat one side of each slice of bread with the margarine. Top the uncoated side of one slice with the desired filling, such as the I Cannot Tell a Lie Cherry or Under the Apple Tree fillings that follow, or even favorite pizza ingredients, such as sauce, vegan cheese or nutritional yeast, onions, bell peppers, banana peppers, mushrooms, and so on. Cover this filling or mixture with the other slice of bread, margarine-coated side facing up. Using a mountain pie maker sprayed with nonstick cooking spray, place the pie in the pie maker and close it, locking it in place. Put the pie maker directly into red-hot coals. The cooking time will vary on the heat, so check the pie often, every few minutes, cooking until the bread is toasted and hot.

YIELD: 1 mountain pie

i cannot tell a lie cherry filling

In a large bowl, combine all the ingredients and let the mixture stand for 15 to 20 minutes before using.

YIELD: About 8 servings

under the old apple tree filling

In a large, heavy saucepan, combine the apples, cider, lemon juice, and cinnamon stick. Cover and simmer, stirring often, over low heat until tender but not mushy, about 20 minutes. Stir in the sugar, optional ginger and mace, and nutmeg. Cook, stirring, until the sweetener is dissolved and blended, about 1 minute. Remove from the heat. Discard the cinnamon stick. Pass the mixture through an immersion blender, to control the chunkiness of the apple filling. In addition to being a mountain pie filling, this can also be served warm or chilled as a side dish of applesauce.

YIELD: 4 to 6 servings

CHERRY FILLING

5 cups pitted sour cherries (2 to 2½ pounds)

1 cup sugar

3 to 3½ tablespoons quick-cooking tapioca

2 tablespoons water

1 tablespoon strained freshly squeezed lemon juice

½ teaspoon vanilla extract

3 tablespoons chilled vegan margarine, cut into small pieces

2 tablespoons vegan egg substitute

APPLE FILLING

3 pounds apples, cut into ½-inch-thick slices

½ to ¾ cup cider or apple juice, depending on the juiciness of the apples

1 to 1½ tablespoons freshly squeezed lemon juice

1 large cinnamon stick

Scant ½ cup sugar

1 teaspoon ground ginger (optional)

1 teaspoon ground mace (optional)

½ teaspoon ground nutmeg

1 pint fresh strawberries, stemmed and well washed

Canola oil for coating the berries

Vegan ice cream or sorbet of choice (Vanilla, I Scream! recipe follows)

VANILLA, I SCREAM!

½ cup vegan cream of coconut, such as Coco Lopez

1 cup soy milk or other vegan milk

½ cup sugar

8 ounces silken tofu

1 tablespoon vanilla extract

Seeds scraped from ½ vanilla bean (wrap and refrigerate the other ½ bean for another use)

2 to 3 tablespoons vanilla-flavored vodka

Strawberry Skewers with Vanilla, I Scream!

This dish might just prove that redheads do have more fun. When a skewer of grilled strawberries is paired with a favorite vegan ice cream, such as the vodka-infused Vanilla, I Scream!, which is making a cameo appearance here from *The Tipsy Vegan*, or a sorbet, you'll never get your guests to leave.

Thread the strawberries onto skewers (presoak the skewers in water for 20 to 30 minutes if using bamboo). Brush with canola oil and grill for 3 to 4 minutes, turning occasionally, just long enough to create grill marks on the fruit.

Serve with a scoop or two of your favorite vegan ice cream or sorbet.

YIELD: 3 or 4 servings

vanilla, i scream!

In a standing blender, combine all the ingredients, blending until thoroughly pureed. Pour the mixture into an ice-cream machine and freeze according to the manufacturer's instructions. Transfer to the freezer and freeze for at least 3 hours.

YIELD: About 3 cups of ice cream

Grilled Pineapple Rings with Sorbet

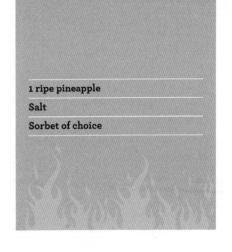

1 ripe pineapple

Salt

Sorbet of choice

To select a ripe pineapple, especially when they're at their best during summer, use your nose to lead you to the real scoop on this ornamental fruit. It should smell as sweet as a fresh breeze. Then, let your grill do the rest of the work, adding its charred signature to the hearty tropical favorite.

Make sure the grates are well oiled, and then heat the grill to medium.

Cut off the top and bottom of the pineapple and trim all the skin from around the sides. Cut the pineapple into rings or wedges. Sprinkle a little salt over the fruit and grill for 8 to 12 minutes, turning once.

Serve with a sorbet of choice.

YIELD: 4 servings

1 (16-ounce) package sweetened frozen raspberries, thawed

¼ teaspoon powdered ginger

2 tablespoons Cointreau (optional)

8 strawberries, halved

4 peaches, halved or quartered

8 chunks pineapple

4 papayas, plums, or nectarines, halved

¼ cup balsamic vinegar

2 teaspoons sugar

Note: If you can't find frozen raspberries, substitute frozen strawberries. As always, if you're using bamboo skewers, soak them in water for 20 to 30 minutes before threading on the fruit.

Tropical Kebabs with Raspberry & Cointreau Dip

Ever dreamed of being a castaway far from the hustle and bustle? Only you and your grill millions of miles away from civilization. Me, too! Well, then, consider your grill an island unto itself and this skewered line-up of strawberries, peaches, pineapple, and papayas with a raspberry and Cointreau dip your first-class ticket to paradise.

In a blender, purée the raspberries, ginger, and Cointreau until smooth. Refrigerate for 2 hours before you begin grilling the fruit.

Make sure the grates are well oiled, and then heat the grill to medium.

When you're ready to grill, thread pieces of the fruit onto eight skewers, alternating the fruit as you wish. In a small bowl, whisk together the balsamic vinegar and sugar.

Grill the fruit until lightly browned, turning frequently and brushing with the vinegar mixture during grilling.

Serve the grilled fruit with the raspberry dip on the side.

YIELD: About 8 servings

Chapter 12

GRILLSIDE HAPPY HOUR

The trio of sunshine, grilling, and a round of drinks is as obvious as water in the ocean or trees in the forest. Just as this book redefines what grilling is, here it also revitalizes the concept of Happy Hour, making it a family-friendly time with a rip-roaring selection of cocktails and nonalcoholic (NA) thirst quenchers—classic summertime throwbacks mixed with playfully modern refreshers.

Full of bar favorites like an array of flavored rums, liqueurs, wine, vodka, schnapps, Southern Comfort, and champagne as well as stand-alone sweet teas, lemonades, and tropical combinations using pineapple, orange, watermelon, apple, lemon, and lime juices with colorful garnishes, this grillside collection will suit all your guests' tastes no matter their age or preference. These drinks are meant to reflect how like grilling itself, or Happy Hour, for sure, summer is as much a state of mind as it is a time when anything is possible.

Of course, I would never discourage you from simply rolling out a good ole case of ice-cold beer, which has always been the original nectar of the grilling gods and goddesses.

6 ripe strawberries, stemmed
and sliced thinly

⅓ cup blueberries

¼ cup sugar

¼ cup grenadine or crème de cassis
(a sweet, dark red liqueur made
from blackcurrants)

1 tablespoon freshly squeezed
lemon juice

1 tablespoon freshly squeezed
lime juice

2 tablespoons freshly squeezed
orange juice

2 teaspoons freshly grated orange zest

3 (12-ounce) bottles of your favorite
beer

Six-Pack Punch

This fruity beer punch has a special knack for fueling those of us who like to prowl the party scene in a pack. When your favorite lager is mixed with lemon, lime, and orange juices, fresh strawberries and blueberries, and grenadine, it's game on! With all the flavored beers and homebrews out there, you can switch-up this celebratory punch whenever you want for an original party pleaser every time.

In a large bowl, combine all the ingredients, except the beer, and stir until the sugar is dissolved. Cover the bowl with plastic wrap and refrigerate for several hours to overnight, stirring every so often to blend the flavors. Meanwhile, chill six 20- to 24-ounce glasses.

When serving time arrives, give the juices a final stir and divide the mixture among the six chilled glasses. Then pour 6 ounces of beer into each glass, stir lightly, and serve at once.

YIELD: 6 servings (a.k.a. a six-pack of beer punch)

Sweet Tea NA

This Southern classic really hits the spot on a hot summer's day, and with a few splashes (or more) of golden rum, on a hot summer's night.

Choose a heatproof 8-cup glass pitcher. Pour in the boiling water and add the baking soda and tea bags. Cover and let steep for 20 minutes.

Pull out the tea bags and discard them. Stir in the sugar until it dissolves, then add the cool water. Refrigerate until cold.

Serve over ice with or without golden rum or vodka, to taste. Garnish with the lemon slices.

YIELD: 6 to 8 servings

2 cups boiling water

Pinch of baking soda

7 tea bags, any paper or string removed

⅔ cup sugar, preferably superfine

6 cups cool water

Golden rum or vodka (optional)

6 to 8 lemon slices, for garnish

The July Martini with Strawberries & Honeydew Melon

1 cup vodka

1 teaspoon strawberry liqueur, or to taste, or a splash of sloe gin

10 strawberries, halved

10 scoops honeydew melon, made with a melon baller

For as long as I can remember, I've searched for the secret to making July last forever. Thanks to vodka's talent for blending seamlessly with fruit, especially these strawberries and honeydew melon balls, I just found it!

Fill a cocktail shaker with ice. Pour in the vodka and strawberry liqueur. Shake well for 2 minutes.

Divide the halved strawberries and melon scoops among four 8-ounce tumblers. Shake the vodka mixture one more time, then divide the vodka among the four tumblers.

YIELD: 4 servings

4 teaspoons grated zest, plus ½ cup juice from 2 to 3 medium-size limes

4 teaspoons grated zest, plus ½ cup juice, from 2 to 3 medium-size lemons

¼ cup white grapefruit juice

¼ cup superfine sugar

Pinch of salt, plus additional salt for rimming the glasses (optional)

2 cups crushed ice

1 cup 100% agave tequila, preferably reposado

1 cup triple sec

A Pitcher of Margaritas

For this crazy-cool pitcher of margaritas, the longer the zest and juice mixture steeps, the better. But if you're in a hurry to get the show started, omit the zest, skip the steeping process, and drink a toast to living life in the fast lane.

In a 1-quart glass measuring cup, combine the lime zest and juice, lemon zest and juice, grapefruit juice, sugar, and the pinch of salt. Cover with plastic wrap and refrigerate until the flavors meld, for 4 to preferably 24 hours.

Divide 1 cup of crushed ice among four to six margarita glasses. Strain the juice mixture into a 1-quart pitcher or cocktail shaker. Add the tequila, triple sec, and remaining crushed ice. Stir or shake until thoroughly combined and chilled, 20 to 60 seconds. Pour or strain into the ice-filled glasses. Serve immediately.

YIELD: 1 quart, serving 4 to 6

Bowl of Bubblies

No need to save champagne just for holidays or special events, nor is there any need to use super-expensive bubbly in this sparkling punch. This Bowl of Bubblies works equally well for ringing in the New Year or when laughing your way through an afternoon around the grill with family and friends.

In a large, nonreactive punch bowl, stir the pineapple-orange concentrate with the lemonade concentrate. Pour in the ginger ale, champagne, and club soda. Add a dozen or more ice cubes and promptly ladle into punch glasses.

YIELD: 9 to 12 servings

1 (12-ounce) can frozen pineapple-orange juice concentrate, thawed in the can (see note)

1 (6-ounce) can frozen lemonade concentrate, thawed in the can (see note)

1 (12-ounce) can ginger ale, thoroughly chilled

1 (750 ml) bottle champagne

2 cups club soda, thoroughly chilled

Note: *The quickest way to thaw frozen juice concentrate (or most anything else frozen) is to let it sit under running cold water.*

Mojito Mojo

This traditional Cuban highball with white rum and muddled mint leaves packs a surprising wallop, so be sure to have a few snacks nearby—and adequate space to cha-cha-cha under the stars until dawn.

In a thick 8-ounce glass, place the mint leaves and one lime wedge. Use a muddler or thick wooden spoon to crush the mint and lime together. Add two more lime wedges and the sugar and muddle again. Add the ice and pour the rum over the ice. Fill the rest of the glass with the seltzer water. Stir and taste for sweetness, adding more sugar if desired. Garnish with the last lime wedge.

YIELD: 1 serving

12 fresh mint leaves

1 small lime, carved into 4 wedges

2 tablespoons sugar (more may be needed)

1 cup ice cubes

2 ounces white rum

½ cup seltzer water

PRETTY IN PINK FLAMINGO

½ ounce Southern Comfort

½ ounce coconut-flavored rum

Splash of pineapple juice

Dash of grenadine

Dash of freshly squeezed lemon juice

**FROZEN TOOTIE FRUITY
GOOD MOODY CUTIE**

1 (6-ounce) can frozen orange juice,
thawed

1 (6-ounce) can frozen lemonade,
thawed

6 ounces water (use can from
lemonade to measure)

¼ to 1 cup sugar

1 (8 ¾-ounce) can crushed pineapple

12 ounces ginger ale

6 bananas, sliced thinly

12 to 15 maraschino cherries
(optional)

Pretty in Pink Flamingo

You're about to find out why flamingos have more fun than the rest of us.

In a shaker half-filled with ice, combine all the ingredients, shaking well. Pour into a cocktail glass of choice.

YIELD: 1 serving

Frozen Tootie Fruity Good Moody Cutie NA

You can't help but have a smile on your face while drinking this good mood juicer that pulls double duty as a party icebreaker or a light after grilling dessert with a cherry on top.

In a container, combine all the ingredients, except the bananas and cherries, stirring to mix. Layer the bottoms of twelve or more cups with the bananas. Evenly pour the mixture into the cups. Drop one cherry into each cup, or wait until just before serving. Freeze the mixture. Remove the cups from the freezer 30 to 40 minutes before serving.

YIELD: 12 to 15 servings

Tiki Mai Tai

With its Polynesian flair and long history, including a famous feud over who created the original and later its having a starring role in Elvis Presley's *Blue Hawaii,* it should come as no surprise that the root meaning of *mai tai* is "good." So, ignite those torches, slip on those grass skirts, and cue the rolling waves of rum, orange liqueur, and tropical juices.

In a shaker, combine all the ingredients with ice, except the dark rum, cherry, and pineapple slice, shaking well. Strain the mixture into a highball glass filled halfway with ice. Top with the dark rum and garnish with the cherry and pineapple slice.

YIELD: 1 serving

1 ounce light rum

½ ounce triple sec

¼ ounce freshly squeezed lime juice

1½ ounces pineapple juice

1½ ounces freshly squeezed orange juice

Dash of grenadine, or more to taste

½ ounce dark rum

Maraschino cherry, for garnish

Pineapple slice, for garnish

ISLAND ZOMBIE

¼ cup gold rum

2 tablespoons white rum

2 tablespoons dark rum

2 teaspoons apricot liqueur

2 tablespoons pineapple juice

2 tablespoons freshly squeezed
orange juice

1 tablespoon freshly squeezed
lime juice

1 teaspoon sugar

BACKYARD KAMIKAZE

1 part vodka

1 part triple sec or Cointreau
(replace with blue curaçao to make
a Backyard & Blue Kamikaze)

1 part freshly squeezed lime juice
(replace with raspberry liqueur to
make a Raspy Backyard Kamikaze)

Island Zombie vs. Backyard Kamikaze

It's a battle of edible proportions. And the fate of your thirst hangs in the balance. Will it be the rum and fruit juiced Zombie your guests prefer or the vodka and orange-wielding Kamikaze? Once you unleash them grillside, it's really out of your hands. But the good news is, no matter which prevails, you will always be the ultimate winner when serving up these party monsters.

island zombie

In a shaker filled with ice, combine all the ingredients, shaking well. Strain the mixture into a tall glass. Garnish with fruit slices of choice.

YIELD: 1 serving

backyard kamikaze

In a shaker filled with ice, combine all the ingredients, shaking well. Strain the mixture into a glass. A cherry on top will definitely score bonus points.

YIELD: 1 serving

BLEEP! on the Beach

There are many different ways to make BLEEP! on the Beach. In fact, you really can't screw it up. Have fun playing around with the ingredients, maybe by adding a little more vodka and peach schnapps while reducing or forgoing the triple sec and melon liqueur. Or, you can play it safe and eliminate the alcohol, combining equal parts cranberry juice, grapefruit juice, and peach nectar, all topped with a cherry and other garnishes. Anyway you do it, you're bound to be left all aglow.

In a shaker, combine all the ingredients, except the garnishes, and shake well. Strain into a highball glass and garnish with the orange and pineapple slices and cherry. Or fill a tall glass with ice, layer the ingredients, stir, and garnish.

YIELD: 1 serving

½ ounce vodka, or coconut-flavored rum

½ ounce triple sec

½ ounce peach schnapps

½ ounce melon liqueur

2 ounces freshly squeezed orange juice, or to taste

2 ounces pineapple juice, or to taste

Splash of cranberry juice

Splash of amaretto (optional)

Ice

Orange and/or pineapple slices, for garnish

Maraschino cherry, for garnish

1 cup sugar

4 to 5 cups water

6 to 8 lemons, for juicing and garnishing

Garnishes: fresh strawberries, blueberries, peach slices, lemon slices, orange slices, banana slices, and raspberries

Lemonade Stand (NA)

This pitcher of liquid gold is all about the bling, namely the kaleidoscope of fruity garnishes that make the lemony refresher look as if you caught a rainbow in a glass. Either add the garnishes yourself, or set them out in small, clear glass bowls and let your guests have fun decorating their own drinks. For an extra touch of flavor, add one large sprig of fresh rosemary to the simple syrup mixture, boil for 3 minutes, and then strain through a fine mesh sieve before combining it with the lemon juice.

In a small saucepan, create a simple syrup by combining the sugar and 1 cup of the water over medium to high heat, stirring until the sugar is dissolved.

Juice five to six of the lemons to get 1 cup of lemon juice. Remove any seeds, but keep the pulp.

In a large, clear glass serving pitcher, combine the lemon juice and simple syrup. Add the remaining water to desired taste. Refrigerate for 30 minutes to 1 hour. Add more lemon juice and/or sugar for desired taste.

Serve the lemonade chilled in tall clear glasses and garnished with your choice of fresh strawberries, blueberries, peach slices, lemon slices, orange slices, banana slices, and raspberries, on the edge of the glass, skewered, and/or floating.

YIELD: 6 to 8 servings

DREAMBOAT

½ ounce rum

½ ounce coconut-flavored rum

½ ounce grenadine syrup

1 ounce freshly squeezed orange juice

1 ounce pineapple juice

1 cup crushed ice

Pineapple chunks, for garnish

AFTERNOON MINT TEA

1½ ounces peppermint schnapps

1 cup tea (freshly brewed)

Ice

Sprig of mint, for garnish

Dreamboat

Coconut. Flavored. RUM! The only thing this tropical dreamboat requests of you is to lay back, relax, and enjoy the ride.

In a blender, combine all the ingredients, blending well until the mixture is like a slush. Pour into a large glass and garnish with a decorative little umbrella and pineapple chunks.

YIELD: 1 serving

Afternoon Mint Tea

Cool down on those steamy hot days while grillside by pampering your palate with this spiked burst of minty coolness. It's also especially exhilarating if you choose to drink your dessert. After-dinner mint, anyone?

In a glass pitcher, combine the peppermint schnapps and tea, blending well. Pour into a large ice-filled glass and garnish with the sprig of mint.

YIELD: 1 serving

Jersey Shore

The beauty of this buff cousin to the Long Island Iced Tea is its chameleon-like ability to adapt to its surroundings. For instance, to make a Long Beach, exchange the Jägermeister for cranberry juice; a Tennessee Jack uses Jack Daniel's instead of tequila; a SoCal trades Jägermeister for OJ; and for a 90210, the Jägermeister is out and champagne is in!

In a tall glass filled with ice, combine all the ingredients, except the Jägermeister and lemon slice. Pour the mixture into a shaker, shaking once. Pour the mixture back into the glass. Add the Jägermeister. Garnish with the lemon slice.

YIELD: 1 serving

1 part vodka

1 part tequila

1 part rum

1 part gin

1 part triple sec

1½ parts sweet-and-sour mix

Splash of Jägermeister

Lemon slice, for garnish

Sassy Sangria

You'll happily float away with this chic sangria and its bold concoction of fruit, brandy, Cointreau, and red wine.

In a large glass pitcher, stir together the lemon juice, orange juice, passion fruit pulp, lemonade concentrate, brandy, Cointreau, and red wine.

Drop in the lemon, lime, and orange rounds and the cherries and give the mixture another stir.

Chill in the lowest part of your refrigerator for 4 hours or, better, overnight.

When you're ready to serve, add the optional club soda and bitters and stir again. Pour into chilled glasses, or serve over ice.

YIELD: 6 servings

¼ cup freshly squeezed lemon juice

½ cup freshly squeezed orange juice

½ cup frozen passion fruit or mango pulp, thawed

½ cup frozen lemonade concentrate, melted

½ cup brandy

½ cup Cointreau

1 (750 ml) bottle dry red wine

1 lemon, sliced into thin rounds

1 lime, sliced into thin rounds

1 orange, sliced into thin rounds

½ cup pitted cherries, fresh or canned

1½ to 2 cups club soda (optional)

A few dashes of Angostura bitters (optional)

Note: This will make six 1-cup servings, but it's easily doubled!

Tipsy Blueberry Bush

TIPSY BLUEBERRY BUSH

2 ounces triple sec

2 ounces blueberry-flavored vodka

2 ounces blueberry juice

Ginger ale

Fresh or frozen blueberries,
for garnish

When the blueberry bushes are in bloom, grab your berry bucket, and hit the outside bar. Fresh berries join this sapphire lineup of blueberry vodka and blueberry juice, with a swig of triple sec for good measure.

In a shaker filled halfway with ice, combine the triple sec, blueberry vodka, and blueberry juice, shaking well. Strain the mixture into a cocktail glass. Top with the ginger ale to taste. Garnish with the blueberries.

YIELD: 1 serving

The Spiked Ruby Daiquiri

THE SPIKED RUBY DAIQUIRI

2 ounces light rum

1 ounce freshly squeezed lime juice

6 ice cubes

5 to 6 fresh strawberries, sliced, plus extra for garnishing (use frozen if necessary)

2 teaspoons sugar

½ ounce strawberry schnapps, or to taste (optional)

Lime slice, for garnish

It can be the middle of winter and yet no grilling party is complete without a round of daiquiris. There's just something about the icy-licious marriage of rum and strawberries that takes fun from zero to fabulous in one frosty gulp.

In a blender, combine all the ingredients, blending until the mixture is smooth. Pour into a large, festive glass. Garnish with the extra strawberry slices and lime slice.

YIELD: 1 serving

Happy Camper (NA)

Whether you're five or ninety-five, this sweet punch bowl of fruit juices, ginger ale, and garnishes will make you go all giddy while you play in the sun, waiting for the aroma of charcoal to let you know it's time to chow down.

In a large punch bowl, combine all the ingredients, mixing well. The orange slices, pineapple slices, and cherries can be frozen into a floating ice ring, if desired.

YIELD: 12 to 15 servings

23 ounces freshly squeezed orange juice

23 ounces pineapple juice

23 ounces apple juice

1 (1 L) bottle ginger ale

Ice, as desired

Orange slices, for garnish

Pineapple slices, for garnish

Maraschino cherries, for garnish

6 cups seeded and cubed watermelon

1 cup halved fresh or frozen strawberries

Juice from 3 to 4 lemons, to equal ½ to ¾ cup (remove seeds, leave the pulp)

1 cup sugar

2 to 2½ cups water

Watermelon juice (store-bought; optional)

Garnishes: Fresh strawberries, lemon slices, orange slices, watermelon slices/chunks, and cherries

Watermelon Giggles with Strawberries & Lemon ⓃⒶ

A cheery composition of watermelon, strawberry, and lemon flavors combined with a carnival of garnishes, this is a comfort drink for the whole family that will always make *home sweet home* feel a little closer.

In a blender, combine all the ingredients, except the watermelon juice and garnishes, blending until smooth.

Pour the mixture into a large, clear glass serving pitcher and refrigerate for 30 minutes to 1 hour. Add the optional watermelon juice, more water, and/or sugar, to taste, if desired.

Serve chilled in tall clear glasses and garnished with your choice of fresh strawberries, lemon slices, orange slices, watermelon, and cherries, on the edge of the glass, skewered, and/or floating.

YIELD: 6 to 8 servings

3 pints fresh strawberries or frozen
strawberries

1¾ cups freshly squeezed orange juice

½ cup freshly squeezed lemon juice

1 cup sugar

Strawberry Ice NA

This crystallized sweetheart will cool you off as a colorful drink around the picnic table or as an all-natural reinvention of the snow cones we devoured as children, especially when heaped into a paper cup sans vodka or ginger ale.

In a food processor or blender, mix the strawberries until smooth. Remove the strawberry mixture from the processor, place it in a large bowl, and add the remaining ingredients, stirring to combine. Pour the strawberry mixture into a 9 by 13-inch baking dish. Place the mixture in the freezer for at least 3 hours to a day before serving. To serve, once frozen, let the mixture set out of the freezer for about 10 minutes. Scoop the mixture into a glass with your favorite beverage, either alcoholic (e.g., vodka) or nonalcoholic (e.g., ginger ale).

YIELD: 20 servings

Watermelon Bikini

Smooth, succulent, and refreshing, the voluptuous watermelon has officially transformed the martini into a whole new eye-popping, tongue-waving summer spectacle.

In a shaker, combine all the ingredients, except the garnishes, with ice. Shake and strain into a martini glass. Garnish with two side-by-side watermelon slices and the frozen berries.

YIELD: 1 serving

G & T on the Docks

Sometimes we need to be reminded that it is the simplest things that bring us the greatest pleasure in this life. Here, a little gin, some tonic water, a few ice cubes, and a lime wedge come together to remind us it's time to find that old, familiar wooden dock where we can sit back, laugh, and wonder how the other half lives.

In a highball glass filled with ice cubes, combine the gin and tonic water, mixing well. Garnish with the lime wedge.

YIELD: 1 serving

WATERMELON BIKINI

2 ounces watermelon juice, or to taste (store-bought or homemade by blending chunks of seedless watermelon until juiced, straining if necessary)

1½ to 2 ounces vodka

2 ounces cranberry juice, or to taste

Splash of pineapple juice

2 watermelon slices and frozen berries, for garnish

G & T ON THE DOCKS

2 ounces gin

5 ounces tonic water

1 lime wedge

Peachy Keen Iced Tea (NA)

A peachy twist on a front porch classic that is perfect for those long lazy afternoons when visions of grilling and mischief are dancing in your head.

In a small saucepan, create a simple syrup by combining the sugar and 1½ cups of the water over medium to high heat, stirring until the sugar is dissolved. Set aside to cool.

In a medium-size saucepan, bring the remaining 5 cups of water to a boil, remove from the heat, and add the tea bags, allowing them to steep for 10 to 15 minutes, or longer until desired strength and color. Remove the bags and cool the tea in the refrigerator for 15 to 30 minutes.

Using a food mill or blender, puree the peaches, then strain through a fine sieve/strainer.

In a large, clear glass serving pitcher, combine the simple syrup, tea, and peach puree, stirring well. Add more water, if needed for desired taste and consistency.

Serve the tea in tall clear glasses and garnish with the skewered peach slices.

YIELD: 4 to 6 servings

1½ cups sugar

6½ cups water

4 regular or green tea bags of choice (peach or orange flavored, if desired), any paper or string removed

1 pound peaches, peeled and pitted

Skewered peach slices, for garnish

Metric Conversions

- The recipes in this book have not been tested with metric measurements, so some variations might occur.

- Remember that the weight of dry ingredients varies according to the volume or density factor: 1 cup of flour weighs far less than 1 cup of sugar, and 1 tablespoon doesn't necessarily hold 3 teaspoons.

GENERAL FORMULA FOR METRIC CONVERSION

Ounces to grams	ounces × 28.35 = grams
Grams to ounces	grams × 0.035 = ounces
Pounds to grams	pounds × 453.5 = grams
Pounds to kilograms	pounds × 0.45 = kilograms
Cups to liters	cups × 0.24 = liters
Fahrenheit to Celsius	(°F − 32) × 5 ÷ 9 = °C
Celsius to Fahrenheit	(°C × 9) ÷ 5 + 32 = °F

VOLUME (LIQUID) MEASUREMENTS

1 teaspoon = ⅙ fluid ounce = 5 milliliters

1 tablespoon = ½ fluid ounce = 15 milliliters

2 tablespoons = 1 fluid ounce = 30 milliliters

¼ cup = 2 fluid ounces = 60 milliliters

⅓ cup = 2⅔ fluid ounces = 79 milliliters

½ cup = 4 fluid ounces = 118 milliliters

1 cup or ½ pint = 8 fluid ounces = 250 milliliters

2 cups or 1 pint = 16 fluid ounces = 500 milliliters

4 cups or 1 quart = 32 fluid ounces = 1,000 milliliters

1 gallon = 4 liters

VOLUME (DRY) MEASUREMENTS

¼ teaspoon = 1 milliliter

½ teaspoon = 2 milliliters

¾ teaspoon = 4 milliliters

1 teaspoon = 5 milliliters

1 tablespoon = 15 milliliters

¼ cup = 59 milliliters

⅓ cup = 79 milliliters

½ cup = 118 milliliters

⅔ cup = 158 milliliters

¾ cup = 177 milliliters

1 cup = 225 milliliters

4 cups or 1 quart = 1 liter

½ gallon = 2 liters

1 gallon = 4 liters

OVEN TEMPERATURE EQUIVALENTS, FAHRENHEIT (F) AND CELSIUS (C)

100°F = 38°C

200°F = 95°C

250°F = 120°C

300°F = 150°C

350°F = 180°C

400°F = 205°C

450°F = 230° C

WEIGHT (MASS) MEASUREMENTS

1 ounce = 30 grams

2 ounces = 55 grams

3 ounces = 85 grams

4 ounces = ¼ pound = 125 grams

8 ounces = ½ pound = 240 grams

12 ounces = ¾ pound = 375 grams

16 ounces = 1 pound = 454 grams

LINEAR MEASUREMENTS

½ in = 1½ cm

1 inch = 2½ cm

6 inches = 15 cm

8 inches = 20 cm

10 inches = 25 cm

12 inches = 30 cm

20 inches = 50 cm

Grilling Resources

PRACTICALLY EVERYONE HAS nearby sources for purchasing grills and grilling accessories. However, since this is an investment in time and pleasure that's meant to last for years to come, be sure to do your homework. Research different types of grills and accessories, get advice from fellow grillers, and make choices based ultimately on your specific needs.

The following are some grilling resources and brands you can explore in making your decisions about how best to fire up.

BBQr's Delight
1609 Celia Road
Pine Bluff, Arkansas 71601
(877) 275-9591
www.bbqrsdelight.com
Wood grilling pellets

Big Green Egg
3417 Lawrenceville Highway
Atlanta, Georgia 30084-5802
(800) 793-2292
www.biggreenegg.com
Ceramic grill and cooker

The Brinkmann Corporation
4215 McEwen Road
Dallas, Texas 75244
(800) 468-5252
www.brinkmann.net
Charcoal, gas, and electric grills, and accessories

Bull Outdoor Products, Inc.
2483 W. Walnut Ave
Rialto, California 92376
(800) 521-2855
www.bullbbq.com
Charcoal and gas grills

Camp Chef
3985 N. 75 W.
Hyde Park, Utah 84318
(800) 650-2433
www.campchef.com
Grills and accessories

Char-Broil
P.O. Box 1240
Columbus, Georgia 31902-1240
(866) 239-6777
www.charbroil.com
Charcoal, gas, and electric grills

Char-Griller
P.O. Box 30864
Sea Island, Georgia 31561
(912) 638-4724
www.chargriller.com
Charcoal and gas grills, and accessories

DiversiTech
6650 Sugarloaf Parkway
Duluth, Georgia 30097
(866) 474-5572
www.grillpad.com
Grill pads and patio protectors

Ducane
200 East Daniels Road
Palatine, Illinois 60067-6266
(800) 382-2637
www.ducane.com
Gas grills

Fire Wire
C/O Inno-Labs
1610 Wheat Road
P.O. Box 395
Winfield, Kansas 67156
(620) 229-9800
www.firewiregrilling.com
Accessories

George Foreman Grills
C/O Applica Consumer Products
23600 Aurora Road
Bedford Heights, Ohio 44146
(800) 231-9786
www.georgeforemancooking.com
Electric grills

Grills for Boats
2718 Grand Avenue
Bellmore, New York 11710
(800) 754-8754
www.grillsforboats.com
Grills made for boats, and accessories

GrillingAccessories.com
C/O ShoppersChoice.com, LLC
4117 Rhoda Drive
Baton Rouge, Louisiana 70816
(877) 743-2269
www.grillingaccessories.com
Accessories

Holland Grill Company
121 Thomas Mill Road
Holly Springs, North Carolina 27540
(919) 557-2001
www.hollandgrill.com
Charcoal and gas grills, and accessories

iboats.com
170 Election Road
Suite 100
Draper, Utah 84020
(800) 914-1123
www.iboats.com
Grills made for boats, and accessories

Kalamazoo Outdoor Gourmet
11 S. LaSalle Street
5th Floor
Chicago, Illinois 60603
(800) 868-1699
www.kalamazoogourmet.com
Hybrid grills

Kristline Corporation
18 West Passaic Street
Rochelle Park, New Jersey 07662
(201) 845-4710
www.grill4all.com
*Portable gas, charcoal, and electric grills,
    and accessories*

Longleaf Lighter Company
P.O. Box 102
Catawba, NC 28609
(800) 239-6938
www.kindlin.com
*Fatwood Firestarter
(Also visit www.fatwood.com for more
    fatwood sources)*

Minden Grill Company, Inc.
2222 Park Place
Minden, Nevada 89423
(888) 985-2249
*www.mindengrill.com
Gas grills and accessories*

Mr. Bar-B-Q
445 Winding Road
Old Bethpage, New York 11804
(800) 333-2124
www.mrbarbq.com
Accessories

Nature's Own
C/O A. J. Martin, Inc.
51 Graystone Street
Warwick, Rhode Island 02886
(800) 443–6450
www.char-wood.com
Natural lump charwood and smoking woods

Rome Industries, Inc.
1703 West Detweiller Drive
Peoria, Illinois 61615–1688
(800) 818–7603
www.pieiron.com
Mountain pie makers and other accessories

Stōk Grills
1428 Pearman Dairy Road
Anderson, South Carolina 29625
(800) 847–5993
www.stokgrills.com
Charcoal and gas grills, and accessories

The Cover Store
3328 Waypoint Drive
Carrollton, Texas 75006
(866) 889–8896
www.the-cover-store.com
Grill covers

Viking
111 Front Street
Greenwood, Mississippi 38930
(888) 845–4641
www.vikingrange.com
Gas grills

Weber-Stephen Products Company
200 East Daniels Road
Palatine, Illinois 60067–6266
(800) 446–1071
www.weberbbq.com
Charcoal and gas grills, and accessories

Well Traveled Living
716 South 8th Street
Amelia Island, Florida 32034
(800) 766–9633
www.wtliving.com
Charcoal grills, including Yakatori grills

Wendell August Forge
1605 South Center Street
Grove City, Pennsylvania 16127
(800) 923–4438
www.wendellaugust.com
Hand-wrought metal serving trays for condiments

W W Wood, Inc.
P.O. Box 398
Pleasanton, Texas 78064
(830) 569–2501
www.woodinc.com
Natural lump charcoal and grilling woods

Zippo Manufacturing Company
33 Barbour Street
Bradford, Pennsylvania 16701
(814) 368–2700
www.zippo.com
Lighters for grills and other outdoor activities

Acknowledgments

To each of the glowing sparks below, who together ignited this book:

To my parents, Jack and Barb ~ Who never said, "Don't play with fire." Thank you for that, and so much more!

To my agent, Steve Troha ~ Who is a master at rocking the grill with the best of them. Thanks most of all for sharing my vision that life is meant to be a party ~ You. Are. The. BEST!

To Renee Sedliar ~ You are the Pied Piper of editors! I would follow you anywhere.

To the trailblazing team at Da Capo Lifelong, including associate director of editorial services, Cisca Schreefel; copyeditor, Iris Bass; proofreader, Martha Whitt; indexer, Donna Riggs; designer, Megan Jones; editorial assistant, Christine Dore; publicist, Lara Hrabota; and marketing manager, Lindsey Triebel ~ Your dedication and talent for setting off fireworks when it comes to creating the best books, including this one, have illuminated the planet time and again.

To Tom Steele ~ Who generously shared his culinary expertise with me, helping to make this book as fiery as it could be. To call you a genius would be a vast understatement!

To Amy Beadle Roth ~ Whose breathtaking photography lets us practically hear the sizzle and makes the food look like we can eat it right off the page. You're a brilliant artist with an impeccable eye!

To Little Coyote ~ Who always loved to chow down on two of this book's main ingredients, fresh mushrooms and red bell peppers, when he would join me every day for lunch. You will forever be my muse and my coauthor in more ways than I can ever explain.

And, finally, to every two-legged, four-legged, winged, finned, buzzing, and even slithering being whom I meet in my adventures ~ I will forever be grateful that our paths crossed in this lifetime.

Until we meet again, my friends—Keep the home fires burning!

Index

◀ *The Blue Pear (page 133)*

◁ *Grilled Peaches with Raspberry Sauce (page 180)*

Maple-Soy Tempeh over Rice (page 168) ▸

◀ *Shiny Happy Poppers (page 15)*

Tropical Kebabs with Raspberry & Cointreau Dip (page 190) ▶

Vegetables on a Picnic (page 95) ▶